The Materiality of Architecture

The Materiality of Architecture

Antoine Picon

University of Minnesota Press
Minneapolis • London

A portion of this book was originally published as *La Matérialité de l'architecture* (Marseille: Editions Parenthèses, 2018). Abigail Grater provided translation assistance for the English edition.

Published by the University of Minnesota Press
111 Third Avenue South, Suite 290
Minneapolis, MN 55401-2520
http://www.upress.umn.edu

ISBN 978-1-5179-0947-5 (hc)
ISBN 978-1-5179-0948-2 (pb)

Library of Congress record available at https:/lccn.loc.gov/2020023729

Printed in the United States of America on acid-free paper

The University of Minnesota is an equal-opportunity educator and employer.

27 26 25 24 23 22 21 20 10 9 8 7 6 5 4 3 2 1

Matter is heavy; it presses down and wants to spread out formlessly on the ground. We know the force of gravity from our own bodies. What holds us upright and prevents a formless collapse? It is the opposing force that we may call will, life, or whatever. I call it force of form *[Formkraft]. The opposition between matter and force of form,* which sets the entire organic world in motion, is the principal theme of architecture.

—HEINRICH WÖLFFLIN, *Prolegomena to a Psychology of Architecture*

Contents

INTRODUCTION

Matter, Materials, Materiality

How to place architecture? The answer to this question is not obvious. Does architecture concern the general public, many of whom are eager to visit monuments such as the Mont-Saint-Michel, the Taj Mahal, and the Sydney Opera House? People readily acknowledge the contribution of architecture to the atmosphere and beauty of cities. What would Florence be without its cathedral and palaces, or Paris without its Haussmannian apartment blocks, or New York without its skyscrapers? Yet museum exhibitions on architectural subjects attract only modest numbers of visitors, and few architects are known outside the circles of specialists and connoisseurs. Who today makes reference to the spectacular hybridity exemplified in the Gothic-baroque of Jan Santini Aichel's churches? Even key architectural works are far from universally appreciated. Despite the fact that seventeen of his projects appear on UNESCO's list of World Heritage Sites, Le Corbusier continues to have his detractors. He remains, for more than a few, the emblematic author of modernist ugliness.[1]

How to place architecture? All over the world, students flock to schools teaching architectural design, even though the conditions of practice are rendered difficult by professional competitiveness and the need to vie for commissions. At the same time, the history and theory of architecture typically occupy a marginal position in departments of art history, treated more often than not as a subfield of that discipline.

It is a fact that the artistic claims of architecture have long been subject to debate; with its succession of structural rules, building codes, and usage constraints, architecture would seem to occupy an ambiguous position with regard to techniques and practices that have a straightforwardly artistic vocation, such as painting and sculpture (despite the undermining of the latter by multimedia). Indeed, it is precisely this ambiguity—this oscillation between art and science, between aesthetic claims and social purposes—that renders architecture so appealing to new generations looking for careers that are reasonably lucrative while also allowing for the expression of individual creativity.

Architecture, then, is difficult to fathom, and perhaps one of the principal reasons for this is the role that matter plays in its configuration. Above all, architecture is matter that is arranged at a large scale for the purpose of resisting gravity and the elements as well as for beauty and use. As early as the first century BC, the Roman architect and engineer Marcus Vitruvius Pollio, better known as Vitruvius, emphasized the essential qualities of solidity, utility, and beauty in his *De architectura*, the only architectural treatise from antiquity that has survived to this day more or less complete.[2] Architecture is matter that weathers and thus reminds us that buildings live not only in space but also in time.[3] It is matter that remains in ruins, gradually losing the sharpness of its contours, the embellishments carved and sculpted into it, until, following the theories of the sociologist Georg Simmel, it has passed through all the intermediate combinations of legible artifice and finally returns to a pure state of nature.[4] Certainly, painting and sculpture involve matter, but in their cases, the matter arguably has a less weighty and overwhelming presence, for it is far more responsive to intimate fashioning by human hands.

The subject of endless philosophical speculation, matter remains always somewhat enigmatic. It appears as fundamentally indifferent to human goals, even if contemporary authors such as British anthropologist Tim Ingold want us to cooperate with its spontaneous activity.[5] I will return later to this desire to cooperate with matter rather than force it to serve human schemes. Though the idea may be enticing, it is worth noting that it has remained mostly confined to academic circles.

Ruins of the Baths of Caracalla, Rome, early third century AD. Ruination reveals the deep material side of architecture.

Deprived of human intentionality, matter actually often resists those who want to use it, beginning with makers and builders. Bending wood and carving stone are never easy; they require strength and skills. These operations may be interpreted as the result of cooperation—in some respects they are—but they can also be seen as tense encounters, as fights against a stubborn material reality. From John Ruskin to Richard Sennett and Tim Ingold, an enduring intellectual tradition has idealized the work of the hands that model matter, often forgetting how difficult that work is in practice, even if this difficulty, once overcome, becomes a source of joy and pride.[6] Because of its indifference and resistance, matter may seem mute and even inscrutable or opaque, an impression reinforced by its general lack of immediate expressivity. Matter and materials do not address us spontaneously (this is especially true of construction materials like brick and concrete).

Although aesthetic considerations occupy a significant place in the field of architecture, the role of individual expression is far more limited than in other arts because of the unique role played by matter, as if its muteness and opacity contaminate architectural works. The effects that architecture produces are also frequently discreet, hovering somewhere at the brink of the spectator's conscious perception. As the philosopher and cultural critic Walter Benjamin pointed out in his classic essay on art and reproducibility, the experience of architecture generally takes place in a distracted manner. The flaneur portrayed by Benjamin does not always pay close attention to the architectural settings he navigates.[7] This distracted state has been radically reinforced in today's digital world by the spread of smartphones, which people compulsively check while walking along the street, sometimes without keeping an eye on what is unfolding around them.

Despite the distracted way in which we, mere passersby or inhabitants, typically interact with our spatial surroundings—with the exception of a certain number of notable monuments and urban or landscape vistas—architecture still gives the impression that it is aimed at us, and on several levels. To begin with, there is the insistent whisper of a built environment without which human actions would not have quite the same resonance. On this subject, the historian of Islamic art Oleg

Grabar has remarked, in an essay on ornament, that the most profound truth concerning architecture is "that it is always at the service of man, and that it has no other purpose than to adorn his manifold activities, something as simple and prosaic as eating or listening to a lecture and something as glorious as worshiping God or contemplating a work of art."[8] The American architect Louis Kahn echoed this ostensive modesty—this apparent subservience—of an art form that is there to embellish everyday human activity in describing one of his own buildings: the library of the Phillips Exeter Academy in New Hampshire, which opened in 1972. He asserted that a structure of this type becomes meaningful only when "a man with a book goes toward the light."[9] The virtuosity of the spatial treatment is justified by the most immediate reading experience possible—an experience Kahn's architecture is there humbly to enrich. This enrichment is among the factors that make inhabiting or dwelling in buildings pleasurable and even inspiring.

But the insistent whisper of the built environment, which architecture instigates at the limit of what is normally audible, is by no means its only effect. The range of impressions also includes the sense that many architectural works give, as soon as we pay a little more attention to them, of speaking to us—as though masses of brick, stone, concrete, and steel were not inert but actually alive. This impression is particularly evident when we encounter works by architects such as Frank Gehry and Zaha Hadid, who have explicitly sought to capture our attention with their animated geometries. However, a simple house is also able to call out to the onlooker. Like faces that are on the verge of speaking and divulging their feelings, some façades are joyful, almost laughing, while others are dark, even withdrawn. In order to account for these striking effects, eighteenth-century architectural theorists developed a notion of what they termed "character." "The more closely I have looked," wrote Nicolas Le Camus de Mézières in *Le Génie de l'architecture (The Genius of Architecture)* of 1780, "the more I have found that every object possesses a character, proper to it alone." He continued: "We must begin with this principle whenever we intend to arouse emotion through Architecture, when we set out to address the mind and to stimulate the soul, rather than to build simply by piling one stone

Louis Kahn, Phillips Exeter Academy Library, 1972. "A man with a book goes toward the light": through the play of matter, shadow, and light, by managing opacity and transparency, architecture serves human activities such as reading.

on another. . . . Effects and sensations spring from the considered intention that governs the ensemble."[10]

The ambition to animate matter by means of an overall organization instead of merely piling it up, as Le Camus observed with disdain, occupies a place of prime importance in the architectural process. Absorbed in a desire to touch the human soul, architecture has constantly evoked the age-old aspiration to render matter emotive, despite its apparent disregard for human feelings. Nothing seems more foreign to thoughts and emotions than matter envisaged as the mute reality from which things are made. Envisaged in themselves, materials are barely more expressive, despite their properties that point toward possible uses by humans. But architecture seems endowed with the intriguing capacity to humanize matter and materials up to a certain point. In this regard, it is hardly surprising that this most material of art forms is also the one that has fueled daring philosophical speculation, as though there exists a deep resonance between the matter that architecture organizes and the cognition of the mind.

In addition to matter, or perhaps as a consequence of it, language likewise plays an important role in the developments that unfold in the following pages. My intention here is certainly not to reengage with the postmodern ambition to cast architecture as a medium of artistic expression embedded in syntax and vocabulary. Rather, my aim is to explore the implications that result from the desire for self-expression. Simply stated, language functions as an upper limit of this desire—ideally, architecture should have the capacity to address the spectator directly, to "speak" to us, as Le Camus would have it. Yet if this speech act were actually successful, it would cause matter to lose the opacity that is constitutive of the art of building. The entire paradox of the architectural discipline consists in endeavoring to render matter expressive, often to the point of overlooking its stubborn resistance to language as such—even though a significant portion of its expressive power lies precisely in this resistance. This is so because the distance that is continually rehearsed between architecture and words is ultimately more powerful than the effects that result from their coming together. Put another way: architecture must constantly seek to speak, yet, by the same token, it must always fail to do so—much like Sisyphus, forever condemned to push a rock up to the mountaintop only to have it escape his grasp and roll back down to the valley floor every time.[11]

The notion of animation is tied to the way in which architecture seems capable of coming to life, but always in incomplete fashion, since it proves incapable of attaining full expression.[12] While God or nature can transform inanimate matter into living bodies, humans do not manage to do this as efficiently. With regard to architecture in particular, they must accept that piles of stones will never truly have the capacity to speak. In this sense, buildings are akin to Michelangelo's unfinished *Slaves,* sculpted figures only just beginning to break out of their stone prisons. Nothing is more powerful than this incompletion; hence architecture arguably derives its most striking effects from its inability truly to "speak."

In the final analysis, to situate architecture, or to think it, necessarily implies confronting the constant oscillation between the silent obstinacy of matter, its resistance to human endeavors, and the desire to animate it so as to make it communicate. It is this crucial tension that will occupy me here, since it seems to provide a fundamental means of grappling with architecture. It is this tension in particular that allows some light to be cast on architecture's inevitable relationship with matter and materials, or more precisely with what I have chosen to name *materiality.* Matter, materials, materiality: at this stage, more thorough attention to these three concepts will serve to clarify the overall ambition of this book. What do the three terms usually mean, and from which perspective will they be mobilized here?

Matter is the most generic term of the three, the one that philosophers and scientists have used extensively to designate the substrate from which things are made. We have both intimate and distant experience of matter. Matter is everywhere; it reaches our senses, but it remains at the same time an abstraction, since we have to deprive the things that surround us of most of their qualities in order to conceive it. René Descartes famously observed that spatial extension is the only property that remains attached to matter once shape, color, odors, and flavors are removed.[13] Following Albert Einstein's equivalence between mass and energy, as well as quantum physics' probabilistic interpretation of it, contemporary science has developed a different take on the subject. But the everyday experience of matter remains marked by a paradoxical mix of evidence and elusiveness. Matter surrounds us; our bodies, our minds perhaps, are made of it, but it seems at the same time opaque and indifferent. These qualities of matter have constituted a recurring theme in philosophy and literature—think, for instance, of the role they play in Jean-Paul Sartre's novel *La Nausée (Nausea)*.[14] Architecture's ambition is to overcome this opacity and indifference in order to reveal a secret connection between matter and humans.

Materials such as wood, iron, and concrete correspond to matter intimately associated with certain properties, from color and texture to mechanical strength, to name only a few. More important, materials are generally associated with human uses. Some of them, like stone, are given by nature, while others, like steel, are the result of complex, often industrial processes. What materials have in common is that they are mostly defined through properties that can be mobilized to achieve certain goals. These properties may be entirely natural, or they may depend on the way the materials are extracted and/or produced. The history of concrete, for instance, is to a large extent the history of how certain properties (such as resistance to water) have been obtained from a mix of slaked lime, sand, and rubble that did not possess them initially.[15] The properties of materials are, by the way, partly defined by humans through research, experimentation, and subsequent conventions. Here again, concrete provides an excellent example of the role played by research and experimentation in the development of properties such as resistance to water and hardness, the definition of which was not evident at first. Toward the middle of the nineteenth century, research and experiments led to a progressive agreement about the definition of the fundamental properties that would characterize modern concrete. Stated another way: materials and their properties are always socially constructed, at least to a certain extent. Aside from production processes, standards, as the ultimate form taken by human conventions, play an essential role in this construction. Thus, in comparison with matter, materials are a step closer to humans.

The concept of materiality cannot be approached in the same way as the notions of matter and materials, for materiality does not correspond to a preexisting substance without or with definite properties. It usually designates the material dimension of a phenomenon, a thing, an object, or a system *in relation* to human thought and practice. It should not be confused with matter or with materials, for it is relational in its essence. It characterizes the type of rapport that we, humans, maintain with matter and materials, and, more broadly, with the physical world around us, with the phenomena, things, and objects that we perceive as fundamentally material. Within the field of materiality in general, architecture is especially turned toward its visible and even tangible component that falls within the realm of the senses. Architectural design is about imagining how this relation can be both evidenced and modulated in the specific case of a place or a building.

In this book, I will go deeper into the question of materiality as envisaged by the architectural discipline—in other words, into the materiality of architecture. As mentioned earlier, this journey will include reflections on architecture and language as well as on animation, a key aspect of the way architecture attempts to infuse matter and materials with human relevance. But it is important to note from the start that because it is inherently relational, materiality does more than say something about the way we relate to matter and materials. It is inseparable from the way we, humans, understand ourselves through this relation. Indeed, our perception of an external reality populated with material entities tells us something essential about the way we think and act. The main argument that I will follow here is that architecture is concerned with materiality because it engages the question of what it means to be human. Another way to understand this ambition is to turn to the notion of inhabiting or dwelling, the term usually used in translations of Martin Heidegger's famous text "Building Dwelling Thinking."[16] To inhabit a place or a building involves a special relation to a specific space and to the material objects that populate it. This relation enables the inhabitant to better realize who she is.

Materiality does not correspond to fixed and timeless content. The relationship between humans and the matter and materials surrounding them has varied considerably across different periods and societies. It depends crucially on technical, economic, and cultural factors as well as on available materials, tools, instruments, and machines; on the organization of labor; and on scientific and philosophical representations of physical reality. It is not even uniform at a certain moment in history and in a given society. An eighteenth-century English aristocrat did not maintain the exact same relation to the material world as a craftsman who was her contemporary. Rather than trying to stay faithful to a generic and somewhat abstract definition of materiality, I will envisage it as a relation in constant evolution and with variations from one end of the social spectrum to the other.

However, at a given moment in history and in a specific society, some features are common to the various conceptions of materiality to which people subscribe, just as there are shared beliefs, knowledge, and practices studied by anthropologists, sociologists, and historians. Other features are widely debated and, because of their revealing character, are studied also by the humanities and the social sciences. Together, these agreed-upon and contested elements define a field that makes it possible to speak of a prevailing approach to materiality. This approach is not monolithic; because of the controversies and contradictions it encompasses, it is not comparable to the paradigms that the philosopher and historian of science Thomas Kuhn introduced in his classic essay on scientific revolutions to characterize moments of consensus regarding the foundations of a scientific discipline.[17] Rather, it looks like the contrasted picture of the Western "culture of time and space" at the turn of the nineteenth century to the twentieth drawn by the historian Stephen Kern, which revolves around a number of shared assumptions as well as heavily debated issues.[18]

In order for its production to be socially acceptable, architecture usually conforms to the dominant approach to materiality. The evolution of the discipline thus echoes the successive transformations of the latter, albeit with distortions produced by specific design agendas. Another way of making sense of this joint evolution is by introducing the notion of "regimes of materiality," just as the historian François Hartog has sought to highlight the existence of distinct "regimes of historicity" from Greco-Roman antiquity to the present, from the Homeric age to the postmodern condition.[19] Regimes of materiality encapsulate the characteristic features of the prevailing approaches to materiality at certain moments in history, the consensus on which those features are built, and the controversies and contradictions that mark the limits of that consensus. Once such regimes of materiality have been highlighted, various histories of architecture could be rewritten in the light of the successive understandings and, above all, experiences of materiality, of which buildings perforce bear the imprint. Toward the end of this book, I will venture to sketch out such a revised history of Western architecture by considering successively the Renaissance, the turn of the eighteenth century to the nineteenth, and the modernism of the first half of the twentieth century as key episodes in the transformation of the shared conception of materiality. My aim in offering this revision is not to propose a new periodization of Western architecture; it is to understand this architecture from a different perspective than most common interpretations employ.

In order to speculate further on what the evolution of architecture might look like from the perspective of successive regimes of materiality, I will also envisage the transformations that architecture has undergone in the past few decades in view of the spread of digital culture and the rise of environmental issues, two developments that are more closely linked than is often acknowledged. The digital realm is not simply a set of new technologies; it also relates, in particular, to the advent of a culture that reflects a different understanding of materiality. It is important to underscore here that the digital realm has not compromised the materiality of architecture, or relegated it to the virtual and fugitive, as some of the discipline's theorists and practitioners might once have feared.[20] To the contrary, the digital realm has helped to reveal the transformations that affect our contemporary moment. In its most sophisticated form, the architecture of digital avant-gardes is all about these transformations, which concern simultaneously the relationship we have to our physical surroundings and the ways in which we understand ourselves as subjects confronting a new experience of the material world.[21] As abstract as they may sometimes seem, architectural formulations in the digital age refer back to this new experience of the material world, which continues inevitably to contribute to our humanity.

A key point throughout these developments is that our relationship with matter and materials plays a major role in helping us to define ourselves as sentient beings who are at once distinct from the physical environment and inextricably linked to it. In this respect, it becomes possible to speak of the simultaneous construction or coproduction of the human and the nonhuman. Architecture makes a vital contribution to this double task of distinction and collusion, especially with regard to the question of materiality. Among nineteenth-century theorists, John Ruskin was especially sensitive to the intimate relation between materiality and humanity. It permeates his major writings, from the *Seven Lamps of Architecture* to *The Stones of Venice*. His interest in matter, materials, and the way humans relate to them is among the reasons his work has been rediscovered today by digital architects looking for a reconciliation between matter and design.[22] More recently, the link between materiality and humanity has been among the key themes of the phenomenological interpretations of architecture. For instance, it plays a central role in Finnish architect Juhani Pallasmaa's influential essay *The Eyes of the Skin: Architecture and the Senses*.[23] Yet precisely because phenomenology is engrossed in the need to root the discipline of architecture in an original authenticity that is not conditioned by historical time, it offers a philosophical perspective that has transformed materiality and humanity into invariables, as opposed to recognizing what these dimensions owe to history. It becomes crucial to stress instead that both our assessment of the content of materiality and our understanding of our own human condition have shifted considerably from one historical period to the next.

How not to introduce the question of nature at this stage? Despite the attempts of various contemporary thinkers to get rid of it, the reference to nature is constantly resurfacing in human discourses and practices, to the point that it is difficult to disregard what nature has meant in the past and what it still represents today. Most of the contemporary critiques of nature are actually addressed to a fixed, atemporal conception, which is not the one adopted here. More generally, in their desire to overcome what they perceive as false dichotomies, such as the opposition between nature and culture, some social science theorists—Bruno Latour and his followers in particular—tend to forget how instrumental these dichotomies remain for professionals like architects and engineers, as well as for their clients.[24]

Nature conveys usually mixed feelings of unfamiliarity and intimacy. Indeed, humans claim to be distinct from nature, all the while recognizing that they largely belong to it. Nature cannot be explained away simply as a principle of organic evolution or as a collection of mainly nonhuman objects, beings, and phenomena. It includes also the way in which the matter that constitutes both inanimate objects and living creatures appears to be at the same time utterly indifferent to people and so close to them that, under certain conditions, it seems as though it might be addressing them directly. Thus, nature is inseparable from the question of materiality. Like materiality, it possesses a strongly relational dimension. Confronting architecture, then, means confronting also the relationship that we have with the nonhuman kingdom—that kingdom we generally call "nature," whose bounds and content we are constantly redefining through our explorations, discoveries, experiences, and convictions. This is because our vision and experience of nature are no more fixed than our vision and experience of materiality, contrary to what phenomenologists tend to assume. Our vision and experience of nature are shaped and transformed by cultural and historical contexts, by different places and times. While a work of architecture necessarily bears the impression of the particular regime of materiality that prevailed at the moment of its creation, it likewise reflects the corresponding vision and experience of nature.

Let me also mention the link between the materiality of architecture and its political dimension. Ruskin provides a revealing example of how materiality and politics are imbricated in *The Stones of Venice,* the three volumes of which weave together Venetian artistic and political destinies, matter and materials appearing often as mediators between the two. Materiality and politics are connected for at least two reasons. First, things and objects play a fundamental role in the establishment and stabilization of social relations. Second, because it has to do with the way humans understand themselves, materiality is also involved in their political enterprises. In the conclusion of this book I will offer a few reflections on how taking into account the materiality of architecture opens new perspectives regarding architecture's political relevance. I will introduce for that purpose the notions of situation and décor, which encapsulate a type of agency specific to architecture as a production that is inextricably material and symbolic. Though often mobilized, the dichotomy between these two concepts does not apply in reality to architecture. Because of its closeness to matter and its dependence on materials, the architectural discipline may seem initially to be the least expressive of all the arts. But this very apparent lack of expression is what makes it simultaneously, and somewhat paradoxically, the closest to the aspirations of women and men, these creatures who are never entirely certain to be distinct from nature or to belong to it, a conundrum that Aristotle probably had in mind when he famously characterized humans as "political animals."[25]

In addition to the preceding attempt to situate architecture in relation to matter, materials, and materiality, more clarification is necessary, for all three terms have become extremely frequent, often in confusing ways, in today's architectural discourse and practice. Increasing numbers of writings employ the terms, and numerous projects claim to engage at a deep level with the material dimension of design, an engagement that may lie in innovative uses of materials; in new ways to mobilize highly physical features such as shapes, textures, and colors; or in extended uses of the possibilities offered by digital fabrication. To what extent is this book indebted to this broad tendency? In order to convey my intention here precisely, let me begin by unpacking the general context in which the invocation of matter, materials, and materiality has become so pervasive. Through the incantatory use of these terms, architecture is echoing a number of key aspects of contemporary culture, relating in particular to three ongoing evolutions.

The first evolution involves a general interest in the material dimension of the world. This interest is no longer limited to domains such as science and technology, which aim to understand and transform our physical environment, or to disciplines such as archaeology and anthropology, which have always been highly dependent on the study of material artifacts. Such a shift is especially conspicuous in the humanities and the social sciences, with the rise of a series of approaches that claim to engage with matter and the material dimension more forcefully than before, thus breaking with the logocentric dimension of Western thought—in other words, with the privileged status given to language and discourse. Among these approaches, one finds the various versions of the "new materialism" inspired by the philosophy of Gilles Deleuze and Félix Guattari, or theories and methodologies such as actor-network theory or object-oriented ontology, often interpreted as key expressions of a pervasive "material turn."[26] Beyond their differences, these approaches have in common an emphasis on the material dimension of social, political, and cognitive processes, as well as on the agency of matter, things, and objects. The effects of this shift can be felt in architectural scholarship. Beyond the enduring influence of Deleuze's philosophy and the more recent success of actor-network theory and object-oriented ontology, contemporary architectural theorists and historians often display a desire to study more closely how design is grounded in a series of concrete techniques and how things and buildings possess agency of their own.[27]

As for architectural practice, it is sensitive to the profound transformation of the understanding and production of materials that is currently under way. Science is now able to study more deeply than ever before how matter behaves and what can be expected from the intimate associations among various types of materials, such as polymers, ceramics, and fibers. Other practical consequences are based on the integration into materials of sensors and actuators, or artificial muscles. This has led to a proliferation of new materials, called *composite* or *smart,* which are often designed to fulfill specific requirements.[28] Working at a scale barely imaginable fifty years ago, nanotechnologies add to the possibilities for customizing matter. These developments have contributed to a redefinition of the relationship between matter and materials. From this perspective also, matter and materials appear to possess an agency that extends far beyond their traditional properties, as if they were becoming increasingly active instead of being passive elements from which human projects are made. Although the architectural discipline is still making only limited use of composite, smart, and nanotechnological materials, it bears the mark of this new context.[29]

The digital revolution represents a third factor responsible for the heightened awareness of the importance of matter and materials. Initially, the advent of the computer raised anxieties about a possible dematerialization of human life. The development of a virtual realm distinct from the physical was often evoked. This is not what has happened. Digital content has hybridized with physical reality, bits have become imbricated with atoms, thus reinforcing the strategic importance of the latter. In addition, digital tools have led to a keener sensitivity to material effects such as grain, texture, and color. Computers, tablets, and smartphones that enable users to play with these effects are instrumental in this evolution. More generally, they have brought about a renewed appreciation of all kinds of tangible phenomena, a shift that may be described as a change in the dominant conception of materiality.

The three evolutions described above are actually interrelated, and architecture constitutes one of the domains in which they clearly meet. Through authors ranging from Manuel De Landa and Tim Ingold to Sanford Kwinter, and from Bruno Latour to Graham Harman, there are, for instance, strong links between the "new materialism" and the "material turn" experienced by the humanities and the social sciences and the intellectual background that inspires many proponents of the digital avant-gardes in architecture.[30] As for the notion of "material computation" mobilized by designers such as Achim Menges and Jenny

Sabin, it appears at the intersection of the research on new materials and the extensive use of digital tools.[31]

Does this mean that the architectural discipline is experiencing something like a "material turn"? While it bears the mark of the context that I have just evoked, architecture is in fact realigning with the strong material dimension that is evident to anyone who has studied or practiced it. This dimension was never forgotten, despite the concerns of theorists and historians like Kenneth Frampton, who assumed that digital tools would jeopardize the special relation between architecture and matter encapsulated in the notion of tectonics.[32] It has simply become more present and, above all, is now interpreted in different terms than it was at other moments in the history of the discipline.

Because of its inescapable physical dimension, its dependence on matter and materials to carry out its intentions, architecture is confronted with a challenge that appears to be the opposite of the agenda fostered by the proponents of the "new materialism" or the "material turn" in the humanities and the social sciences. For architects are trying to make matter expressive to the point that it may sometimes seem to be about to "speak," whereas philosophers and sociologists want to escape the logocentric tradition of their disciplines in order to rediscover the mute agency of things and objects. On the side of built objects, language has kept its appeal, while today some scholars of the humanities and the social sciences attempt to break with its dominance.

Although language represents an unavoidable reference for architecture, architecture's quest for expression is not ultimately linguistic. As I have argued, its productions are in fact unable to truly speak. Nevertheless, this quest reveals an ambition to move the spectator through highly material means. Such an ambition is characteristic of the discipline insofar as it appears as the most material of all the arts, so material that it can often be confused with mere construction. Other arts may of course mobilize matter extensively, but they are generally not as dependent on matter as is architecture. Sculpture, for instance, may rely on the imitation of existing things and beings to achieve expression, but it is not forced in essence to put matter at its center. It is striking, by the way, how various modern and contemporary artists have borrowed resources from architecture—such as space and structure—when trying to showcase matter and more generally physical phenomena as the core of their work.[33]

The architectural ambition to make matter expressive implies that a connection can be established between matter and humans, a connection that I have chosen to call materiality in this book, where it plays a central role. Again, materiality is not matter. It designates the way humans relate to matter and materials through the prism of their beliefs, knowledge, and practices, architecture being one of these practices—a key one, actually, because of the part played by matter in its very definition. Materiality is neither an idea or set of ideas nor a series of concrete habits and operations. It corresponds to a field where ideas, but also imaginaries, interact with experiences and practices. It encompasses all the elements that contribute to structuring the relation to the material world of a given society at a certain moment in its history. Besides its social dimension, its temporal and dynamic character is essential. Materiality is in constant evolution. The theoretical agenda that inspires this book is inseparable from a historical perspective, which seems to me all the more necessary now that "presentism"—that is, the tendency to be oblivious to the changes brought by time, as if only the present matters, and as if current beliefs are actually timeless facts—has become a pervasive feature of many contemporary debates.[34]

From the historical perspective adopted here, there is no right attitude toward matter and materials, no proper understanding of materiality as opposed to wrong ones. I am thus very far from Tim Ingold's moral injunctions to respect matter's inherent propensity, to compose with it rather than bend it forcefully to human will.[35] Indebted to Deleuze, Ingold's developments are taken here as an expression of a contemporary moment in the history of materiality, not as a long-forgotten truth about matter and materials that should be rediscovered and promoted. This relativistic stance also applies to architecture. The aim of this book is not to foster a specific design agenda, modernist or postmodernist, digital or postdigital. The counterpart of frustrating architects' spontaneous craving for clear-cut doctrines and for gurus promoting them is found, however, in an attempt to elucidate the remarkable ability of the architectural discipline to take into account simultaneously the opacity of matter and the longing of humans to understand who they truly are, an ability synonymous with the power to make matter expressive.

This book is about architecture, but it is also about an issue that extends far beyond the realm of architecture as a discipline. There are two kinds of books on architecture: those whose ultimate ambition is to contribute to the discipline, and those that use architectural questions as a springboard toward other inquiries. Here, beyond the "material turn" of the humanities and the social sciences, architecture is considered as a way to understand how matter and materials, as well as the things and objects that are made from them, are actually constitutive of humans. The logocentric tradition of Western thought has never been able to avoid this question entirely. Conversely, the "material turn," despite its claims to the contrary, has not so far been able to abolish entirely the primacy given to words and discourse.[36] Because of its singular position at the frontier of the nonhuman and the human, the material and the meaningful, because we inhabit it or dwell in it, because its productions shape us, architecture acts as a constant reminder of the limits of language and of the power of things.

1

From Making to Expression

Architecture is a supremely material art. It works on masses of timber, brick, stone, concrete, and steel. The intimate connection that it maintains with natural, bulk, alloyed, and aggregate materials, generally less precious than those mobilized by other artistic practices, has arguably contributed to its placement at the bottom of the pyramid of arts, as though architecture were itself akin to a massive, foundational substructure that nevertheless remains humble in comparison with what looms above it. Consider, for example, the German idealist philosopher Georg Wilhelm Friedrich Hegel's *Lectures on Aesthetics,* compiled posthumously in 1835, in which architecture is positioned as a powerful yet somewhat brutish preamble to the teleological march that leads from sculpture to poetry via painting and music.[1]

More to the point, architecture makes itself manifest as an ordering of the materials that it employs. In so doing, it comes up against "the resistance and obstinacy of matter," to use an expression found at the start of the 1683 treatise *L'Art de jetter les bombes (The Art of Throwing Bombs)* by the French architect and engineer François Blondel, creator of the Porte Saint-Denis in Paris and the royal rope factory at Rochefort. "In a word," wrote Blondel, "and this holds true for all the arts, mere knowledge of the precepts is never enough to achieve perfection. One must know how to apply these precepts to the subject at hand, and it is in this application that one always finds the resistance and obstinacy of matter. This gives rise to a thousand hitherto unforeseen obstacles and hindrances, which can be overcome only through practice and experience."[2] Despite the fact that they have been selected for their properties, which enable them to answer human needs, materials always present some degree of resistance. Ordering them appears at times to be a struggle.

There is no lack of rational elements in this confrontation. In particular, the architect can rely on, then adapt as needed, a corpus of tried-and-tested rules having to do with form, dimensions, and the proper use of materials. Let us designate this fundamentally material component as the "making" of architecture.[3] Nothing seems more removed from the question of expressiveness, not to mention language, than this making of architecture. Extending far beyond the realm of construction, making encompasses the ensemble of know-how and practice by means of which the architect orders matter. A more detailed examination, however, reveals surprising sympathies between the making of architecture and the desire to speak to people. This is utterly clear in the case of the oldest tools used by architects to impose order: the proportional relations of the various elements of construction. When devising the parts of a building, what could be more intuitive than conforming to proportions that have been sanctioned by established use? Proportions possess an almost universal character. They can be found in architectural traditions as diverse as Islamic and Chinese.

In the Western tradition, from the advent of the Renaissance to the onset of the industrial age, an abundant literature has been devoted to the problem of architectural proportions. Both theoretical and practical, this corpus of writings typically adheres to the model of the lengthy exposés that Vitruvius devoted to the subject in his treatise.[4] What emerges from all this is the premise that architectural proportion is never purely technical, even if its origins are found in the first practical rules concerning structural stability—rules that prescribe, for example, the width of piers according to the span of the arch they support, or the height of columns according to their diameter. Early modern engineers knew, for instance, that a bridge arch was to be between four and five times wider than the piers that supported it. Until the eighteenth century, architects and engineers often obeyed such practical rules.[5]

If Vitruvius and those who followed in his footsteps are to be believed, beyond its technical roots, architectural proportion also addresses people, revealing nothing less than the secret order that governs the products of nature or, even, the entirety of creation. It is this cosmological or divine perspective that inspired many architectural theorists from the sixteenth to the eighteenth century—beginning with the Spanish Jesuit scholar Juan Bautista Villalpando—to speculate on the proportions that the God of the Hebrews dictated for the construction of the First Temple in Jerusalem.[6] According to these authors, the Solomonic proportions were in tune with the ultimate mysteries of the universe, and thus constituted the ideal model. The basic ratios used by architects according to the directives established by long-standing practice and theory are thus never more than a pale reflection of this archetype.

The fascination that the golden ratio has held for architects from the earliest antiquity down to the modernist movement stems from a similar intuition about the capacity of architectural proportion to communicate, in enticingly veiled terms, the secrets of the universe. The anthropometric system of proportion that Le Corbusier named the Modulor should be understood as a derivative product of this long tradition—and it is worth reiterating here Albert Einstein's alleged remark to the architect, who was visiting him in Princeton, New Jersey: that, in his opinion, Le Corbusier's visual scale "makes it difficult to do things badly, but easy to do them well."[7] As with the golden ratio and, more generally, the various systems of proportion employed in architecture over the course of the centuries, the Modulor was devised as the bearer of an essential yet mysterious message concerning the order of the material world.

Since such order imposes itself initially on the mind of the designer who fashions matter, and then on the viewer who perceives harmony without necessarily identifying the exact source, it appears to be common to the material world and, simultaneously, to humankind—a bridge between matter and being. In the Vitruvian tradition, proportion

Le Corbusier, drawing related to the Modulor system of proportions, around 1945. Fondation Le Corbusier, D 1389-R. The Modulor system is directly based on the proportions of the human body; it is supposed to act as a mediator between these proportions and the measures of the universe at large.

comes even closer to us by means of the analogy it insistently draws between the proportions of architectural members and those of the human body. Accordingly, the Doric column is inspired by masculine measurements and the Ionic by feminine measurements—and the Corinthian and Composite serve as evocations of, respectively, the figures of a young woman and a young man. In one of the manuscript versions of his major treatise on architecture and engineering, the Italian Renaissance architect and engineer Francesco di Giorgio Martini offered a striking illustration of this analogical principle by inscribing male and female figures within Doric and Ionic shafts, as if to indicate the possible metamorphosis through which the columns might spring to life. The analogy with the human body is likewise foregrounded in Le Corbusier's Modulor, underscoring that the proportions of architecture have never ceased to mediate between macrocosm and microcosm, between the rules of the universe and those that leave their imprint on bodies and minds. In sum, the process of ordering matter through proportion is constantly driven by a desire to express—a desire that is linked to the view that architecture can directly address the spectator, just as one person can call out to another.

The notion of address becomes even more palpable in the case of another principle of ordering matter that gradually emerged over the course of the eighteenth century: the principle of structure, which is sometimes called "tectonics," with reference to German nineteenth-century theoretical tradition.[8] It is worth noting at the outset that this principle, which today appears intuitively self-evident, was not always present in the history of architecture. This is not to say that the buildings of earlier periods did not possess remarkable structural organization; Gothic churches and masterworks of structural ingenuity such as Filippo Brunelleschi's dome for Florence Cathedral testify to the contrary. Yet it was over the course of the Enlightenment that a new way of reading buildings emerged, one that accorded a special status to their mechanical features. This status was first outlined in the teachings of the Venetian architectural theorist Carlo Lodoli, who advocated a functionalist architecture that was "true" to its materials, as well as in the ideas of his compatriot Giovanni Poleni, the physicist and antiquarian

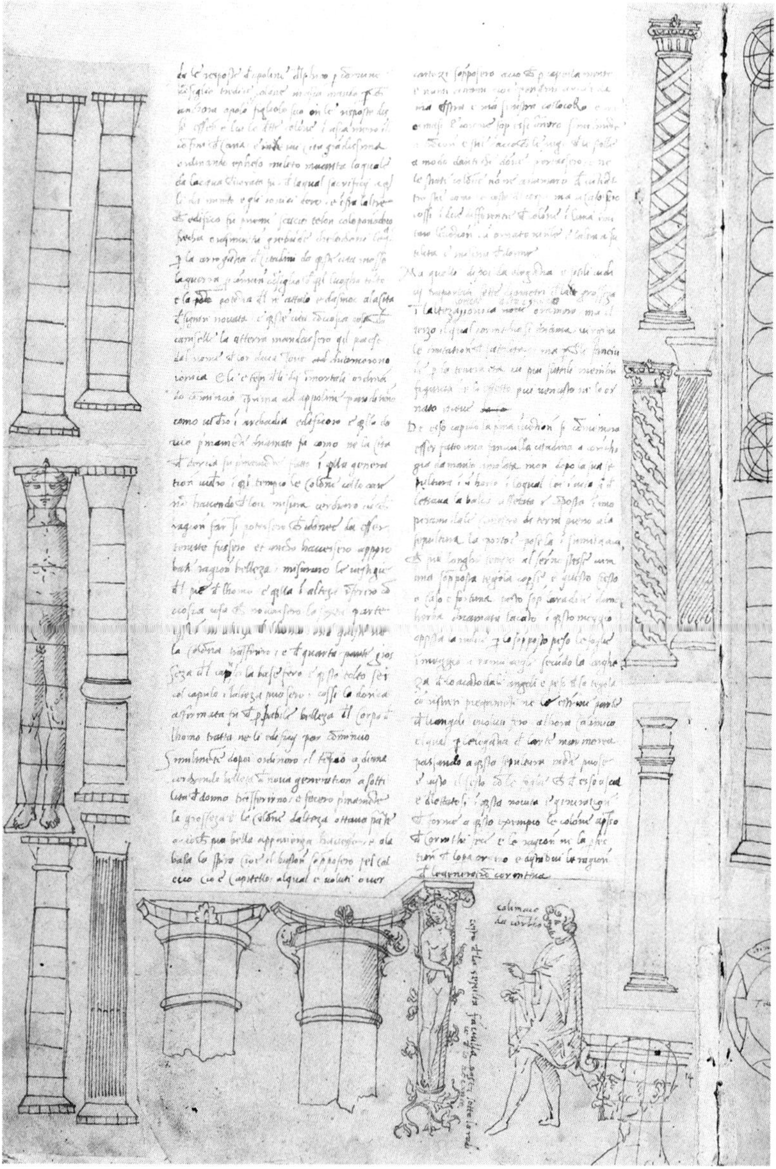

Francesco di Giorgio Martini, *Trattati di architettura ingegneria et arte militare (Treatises of Architecture, Engineering, and Military Art)*, around 1476. Beinecke Rare Book and Manuscript Library, Yale University, MS 491, 13V. A striking illustration of the traditional Vitruvian belief in the analogy between the proportions of the orders of columns and those of the human body.

famous for carrying out in 1748, at the behest of Pope Benedict XIV, a structural analysis of the dome of Saint Peter's Basilica in Rome. Awareness of the structural dimension of buildings developed further in France during the second half of the eighteenth century.[9] It was based on a dynamic vision of the transfer of stresses within matter. Load paths were conceived as a sort of stream running from the top to the bottom of constructions, or from the center to the periphery. This method of reading material behavior led to new kinds of distinctions being drawn between structure, the site of deep flow-like circulation of stresses, and ornament, interpreted as a superficial layer.[10] The load-bearing elements of buildings—pillars, arches, beams, and vaults—now fell irrefutably within the realm of structure, as did the stress transfers that dictated how these elements were assembled. From this moment on, ornament would belong to another domain: that of decoration. The architect Jacques-Germain Soufflot revealed the importance of this distinction, which did not exist in the Vitruvian tradition, when he declared that he would reconcile Gothic lightness with Greek elegance in his new Church of Sainte-Geneviève (now the Panthéon) in Paris. To his mind, lightness was a matter of structural reasoning, while elegance stemmed mainly from ornamentation.[11]

In the wake of the seminal distinction between structure and ornament, other antinomic pairs began to emerge, such as skeleton and skin. These refer to the same fundamental opposition between, on the one hand, the organization of the building (to ensure the correct transfer of mechanical stresses) and, on the other, a set of measures to fulfill other purposes (from thermal insulation to decorative schemes). Their emergence was accompanied by the extension of the structural interpretation of construction to buildings erected before the eighteenth century as well as outside the Western tradition. Hence, one now interprets Gothic cathedrals, Japanese temples, and the men's houses of Papua New Guinea as edifices with *structure,* thus transforming into intemporal evidence a notion that in fact emerged at a certain moment in history, like energy in physics or the genetic code in the sciences of life.

On the face of it, nothing is less expressive than structure, except of course the performance that it achieves and the impression that this performative aspect can give. Large spans and spectacular overhangs can be breathtaking, but in actuality few structures boast such tours de force—and even the most daring structures, such as those designed by engineers, appear sublime in the manner of marvels of nature (like the vertiginous peaks of a rugged landscape) rather than expressive in the usual sense of the term.[12]

Le Corbusier—to refer to him once more—famously played with the apparent impassiveness of ordinary structures in his proposal for the Dom-Ino system, an assemblage of posts and floors that he designed around 1914. This system stands resolutely at the boundary of architecture, where the ambition to communicate with the viewer at a level other than that of structural and programmatic efficiency seems to unravel completely. Yet as the American architect and theorist Peter

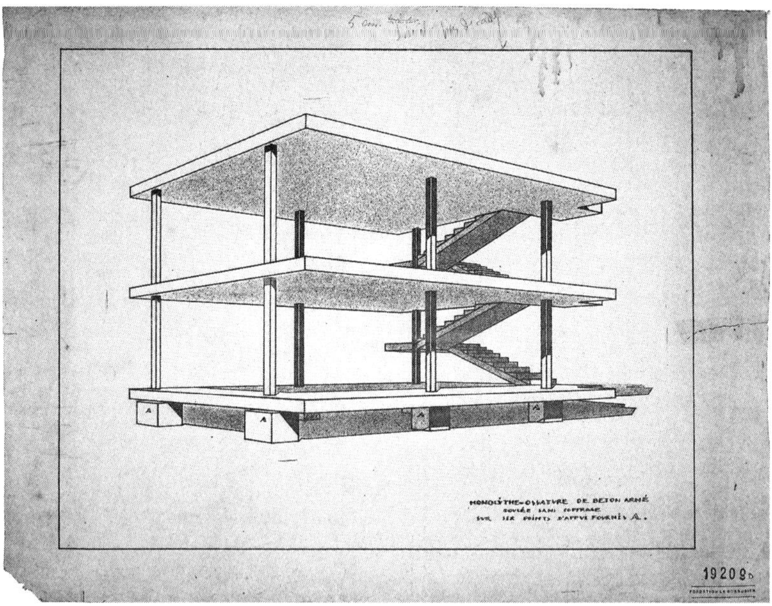

Le Corbusier, perspectival view of the Dom-Ino system, around 1914–15. Fondation Le Corbusier, 19209B. Even at its simplest, as a bare assemblage of posts and slabs, architectural structure is inseparable from expressive concerns.

Eisenman has shown, the Dom-Ino system still manages to insinuate something essential about architecture—that is, its self-referentiality—as a condition of its relationship to humanity.[13] No structure is totally voiceless, even if we might wish for the mechanics of load distribution to remain outside the realm of signification and communication.

To push the implications of this last assertion further, certain structural assemblages have been used as references to the ways in which the mind orders sequences of thoughts and works through the process of reasoning. It is as though some invisible epistemological system based on analogies and connections were casting its net from construction to logic, from structural intuition to the philosophy of mind. Consider here the German poet Heinrich von Kleist, who referred to this type of net or network of analogies and connections in a letter he wrote to his fiancée, Wilhelmine von Zenge, on November 16, 1800. Near a drawing of a vault, Kleist wrote: "Why, I asked myself, does the vault not collapse, given that there is nothing holding it up? Because, I replied, all the stones want to fall down together."[14] Perplexed by the lack of supporting theological or anthropological arguments in Immanuel Kant's philosophy, Kleist saw the vault as a legitimate analogy for the way Kantian critique nonetheless managed to hold the edifice of thought together.[15] A century earlier, the magnificent stability of the vault, perversely borne out by the tendency of individual stones to fall, had already captured the attention of the French academician Charles Perrault, who attempted to enlist it in a manuscript he wrote in his twilight years, probably between 1694 and 1703, in the service of Christian apologetics:

> Nothing offers greater proof of the truth of the Christian religion than the admirable economy of its mysteries, which support each other through their interrelationships. When considered separately, each mystery is painfully incomprehensible, . . . the way they relate to each other makes it easy to concede them. It is as with a stone vault: at first glance, we perfectly understand that it can stand; but when we look only at the stones themselves, one by one, it is somewhat incomprehensible, because of their weight, which seeks only to send them tumbling downward, whereas

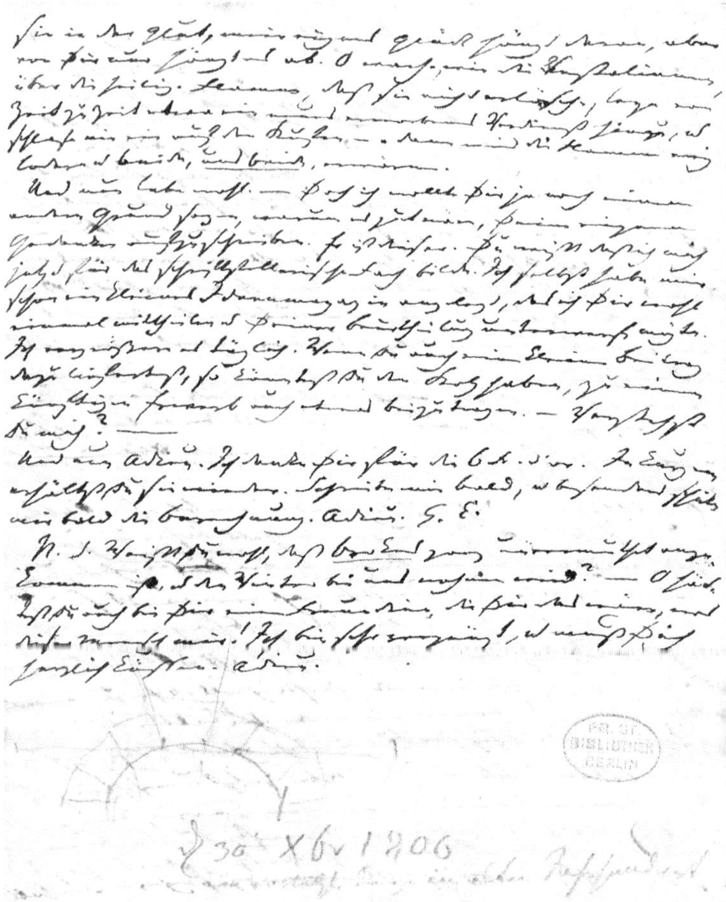

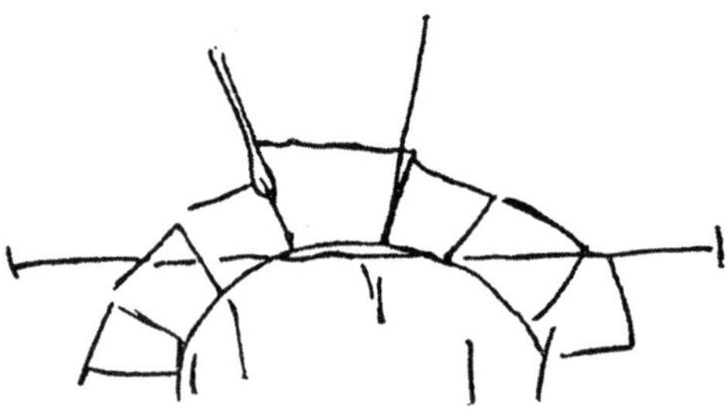

Heinrich von Kleist, diagram of a vault at the end of a letter to Wilhelmine von Zenge, November 16, 1800. Jagiellonian Library, Jagiellonian University, Kraków, Autographen-Sammlung, Kleist. The vault is among the inspiring constructive figures that have often been mobilized by literature and philosophy to shed light on complex intellectual issues.

this same weightiness, when considering the entire structure of the vault, is a justification for and an explanation of why it stands.[16]

From Perrault to Kleist, from Christian mysteries to Kantian metaphysics, there persists a desire to relate the understanding of structures to an interpretation of those far more intangible edifices that are the great religious and philosophical systems—this despite the fact that they are poles apart. Throughout the nineteenth and twentieth centuries, the perception of this complicity between architectonic structures and human thought gave rise to a series of writings that sought to cement the relationship between, on the one hand, the dominant tectonic concepts of a given period and, on the other, the concomitant culture (and here culture is taken in the broadest sense to include the sciences, politics, literature, and philosophy). It was as if an invisible thread, or what the poststructuralist philosopher Michel Foucault famously termed the *episteme,* tethered them together within a single fabric.[17]

The mark of this tethering is palpable, for example, throughout nearly the entire oeuvre of the French architectural historian and theorist Eugène-Emmanuel Viollet-le-Duc, the main protagonist of the current that was subsequently called structural rationalism. In his *Entretiens sur l'architecture (Discourses on Architecture),* published in 1863–72, he offered a whole series of daring parallels: between the ancient Greek way of thinking and the systematic use of the post-and-lintel system, for example, and between the imperial Roman administrative spirit and the erection of formidable masses of bricks relying on the principle of vaulting and the extensive use of an enslaved labor force. He wrote that "the architecture of the Greeks corresponds exactly to the expression of the intellectual state of this people," and he approached Roman construction in the same manner.[18] But to his mind, it was the Gothic in particular that bore triumphant witness to the idea that architectonic structure might serve as the privileged expression of a given civilizational mind-set. For Viollet-le-Duc, Gothic architecture was as much a system of rationales as it was a set of spatial devices and constructional techniques based on pointed arches, slender pillars, and flying buttresses. This explains the title he gave to his most significant work, the

Dictionnaire raisonné de l'architecture française du XIe au XVIe siècle (Reasoned Dictionary of French Architecture from the Eleventh to the Sixteenth Century).[19] "I am sometimes accused of attributing too much to reason," he admitted.[20] He did not repent, however, for an undertaking that left too much room for arbitrariness was a prospect to be avoided at all costs.

At the height of the twentieth century, even as some of the foundational hypotheses of structural rationalism were being wholly dismantled by modernism, the German art historian Erwin Panofsky remained faithful to this type of intuition. In *Gothic Architecture and Scholasticism* (1951), he aligned the spatial and structural organization of cathedrals with the methods of reasoning in medieval philosophy.[21] The driving assumption here again was that structure can express itself as clearly and distinctly as can literature or philosophy. Furthermore, it is precisely through structure that architecture overcomes the obstacle of the muteness of its façade only to prove itself to be more articulate, perhaps even more loquacious, than the other plastic arts.

Yet structure does not speak only to those who know how to decipher both its technical aspects and its cultural logic; it speaks to architects and engineers as well as to scholars and philosophers. If, for the specialists, structure is conjoined to the language of reason and allied to the conceptual realm, it must also operate at a different level, the domain of affect, in order to touch us in the ordinary, quotidian, and individual sense. Here, the role of affect is all the more powerful in the sense that it seemingly precedes any linguistic enterprise and so stands at the threshold between the perceived and the felt, between visual impression and internal sensation. In his *Prolegomena zu einer Psychologie der Architektur (Prolegomena to a Psychology of Architecture)* of 1886, the Swiss art historian Heinrich Wölfflin discussed this prelinguistic capacity to touch the emotions by means of direct appeal to the way in which we sense and understand our bodies—in other words, empathy (a notion to which we will return later).[22] A compelling example of this is the Spanish engineer Eduardo Torroja's 1935 Zarzuela Hippodrome in Madrid, with the striking cantilevers of a grandstand that avoids the sublime manner of the largest civil engineering realizations. As Torroja explained: "It would be a vain undertaking for anyone to try to successfully design a structure without having assimilated, down to the very marrow of their bones, the mechanical principles that govern all the phenomena of internal balance."[23] Completed around the same time, Frank Lloyd Wright's Fallingwater, a house built over a waterfall in rural Pennsylvania, attests to a comparable structural expressiveness; it, too, features impressive cantilevers (if very different from Torroja's) that seem to touch the spectator down to her skeletal core. Wright was an admirer of Torroja's work, which he considered to be an almost perfect illustration of the principles of organic construction.

One should not assume that this expressive capacity should be understood as stemming from the sort of timeless corporeality to which

Frank Lloyd Wright, Fallingwater, view from a low angle near waterfall, 1939. Modernism and its inclination toward structural performance was inseparable from a heroic vision of the body, as if there were an implicit resonance between the play of masses, weight, and void and a proactive stance of the human subject.

phenomenologists, from Alberto Pérez-Gómez to Juhani Pallasmaa, so readily refer.[24] Human bodies, or rather the experience of them, and the images and theories formed from that experience, have varied considerably across the centuries. While we, women and men living today, are still like our most remote ancestors in that we possess a head, two arms, and two legs, some of our intimate sensations are entirely new or now have more prominence than they did in the past; think of how significant the feeling of acceleration has become in our decidedly mechanized society. Other sensations have been diminished by the contemporary world; we have likely become less sensitive to certain natural bodily rhythms, and to the smells and sounds on which our hunter-gatherer ancestors depended for their survival. We no longer experience exactly the same sensations our forebears did, and we do not have the same understanding of ourselves—for instance, we no longer consider ourselves to be hydropneumatic machines, as the seventeenth-century adherents of Cartesianism would have thought; we no longer believe in a vital fluid akin to the electricity that brought Frankenstein's creature to life, unlike those who lived through the first Industrial Revolution; and, as opposed to a more recent generation, we are abandoning the direct analogy between circuits of the brains and those of computers.

In reality, the architectural structures that Eduardo Torroja and Frank Lloyd Wright designed in the 1930s went hand in hand with a modern and willfully heroic vision of the body that is no longer relevant today. The so-called crisis of tectonics and the current call for a renewal in structural thought, as evidenced by contemporary theorists and practitioners such as Neil Leach and Cecil Balmond, should likely be understood in this light.[25] This ostensive crisis is closely linked to the rise of digital culture, and not only because computers are calling into question more traditional approaches in architecture and engineering. The reality is that digital tools are proving inseparable from a far broader transformation of the ways in which people perceive and think about themselves.[26] The current fascination with the theme of the cyborg and the rise of posthumanist doctrines bear witness to this transformation, as do the close connections that have been established between digital technologies and the neurosciences.[27]

Wang Shu, detail of a wall of the Xiangshan Campus China Academy of Art building in Hangzhou, 2002–7. The use of traditional materials recycled from vernacular Chinese architecture contributes to the strong material effect produced by Wang Shu's buildings.

In a pioneering (but not yet published) work, the French art historian Laurent Baridon has outlined a general reflection on the relationships between architecture and the body.[28] This kind of study deserves to be taken up and developed further, most especially where it concerns a potential examination of the evolution of structural and tectonic ideas. When considered from a structural or tectonic vantage point, architectural production does more than simply remind us of the power of technical constraints or assert the clarifying authority of reason. The structural approach, like the search for harmonious proportion before it, also vitally speaks to bodies and the manner in which they allow humans to project themselves into the world in manifold ways.

From the proportions accorded to the elements of construction to the structures that govern load distribution, what seems the most practical in architecture is actually permeated by a quest for expression that proves irreducible to rational problem-solving. This quest often involves the intimate experience of the human body. Prior to the use of tools like proportions and notions such as structures, the mere choice of a material can also be vested with an expressive intention. Think of the role played by the ribbed, bush-hammered concrete in the Yale School of Architecture building by Paul Rudolph, or of the powerful effects produced by the reuse of ancient stones, bricks, and tiles in the Ningbo Museum and the Xiangshan Campus China Academy of Art building in Hangzhou by Wang Shu. These materials convey physical sensations that appeal to the body's capacity to see and touch. The architectural discipline can never be entirely objective. Like matter and the materials that it selects and organizes, the making of architecture appears both distant from and close to us. It usually whispers in our ears, letting us remain in the distracted state that Benjamin associates with the perception of buildings, but it may also, at times, address us more forcefully.

2

Architecture and Language

An Incomplete Encounter

On the path that leads from the mere ordering of matter and materials to the taking into account of materiality, the architectural discipline sees itself inexorably confronted with the issue of expression. To make sense of this encounter, one may be tempted to take an extreme position, asserting that architecture functions as a sort of language. Indeed, language represents the most articulate form of expression, something like an enticing upper limit of the ambition to address humans. What if there were architectural equivalents of vocabulary and syntax, of rhetorical figures and dialectical devices? A question very close to this one has already been raised by Panofsky's intriguing parallel between Gothic architecture and the medieval philosophy of, say, Thomas Aquinas. Without being too literal about such a parallel, it remains interesting to contemplate what kind of relationship may exist between architectural rules and principles, on the one hand, and the structures of language and thought, on the other.

A venerable body of literature, both historical and theoretical, on the subject of architecture and language has tried to explore the links between the two. For example, the late eighteenth century established the terms of what came to be described as *architecture parlante,* or "speaking architecture" (so called by the romantics in their attempt to interpret the didactic geometric purism of the visionary architecture of

Étienne-Louis Boullée and Claude-Nicolas Ledoux).[1] The British architectural historian John Summerson went on to focus on the broader purview of the sixteenth through eighteenth centuries in *The Classical Language of Architecture* (1963), suggesting that Vitruvian-inspired architecture should generally be considered a language with an identifiable syntax and vocabulary.[2] Summerson's assertions served to inspire the Italian historian and critic Bruno Zevi, who, in *The Modern Language of Architecture* (1973), set out to stress "anticlassical" trends, all the while reiterating some of his predecessor's fundamental assumptions. "Even modern architecture," Zevi stated in his introductory remarks, "which emerged in reaction against Neoclassicism, runs the risk of reverting to stale Beaux-Arts archetypes unless it is structured into a language."[3]

However appealing, this type of approach has never found consensus. Detractors point out that architecture is closer to the plastic arts than to discourse, and reticence on the subject is currently so pointed that some theorists and designers reject outright any whiff of the symbolic dimension. Take the architects Jesse Reiser and Nanako Umemoto, for example, who are proponents of the "new materialism" that has coincided with the rise of digital culture; in *Atlas of Novel Tectonics* (2006), they advocate the use of "asignifying signs" because "an architecture that has to explain itself, or be explained, has failed to present its own qualities."[4] In *The Function of Ornament* (2008), the Iranian-born British architect Farshid Moussavi and her coauthor, Michael Kubo, follow this line of thinking when they attribute a "function" to contemporary architectural ornament that would exclude the role of signifier.[5]

Between those two radical attitudes, why not consider language as a constant temptation for the architectural discipline? The stance adopted here consists in recognizing that architecture inaugurates a path toward language, or, more accurately, toward utterance *(parole)*, for in its highest form of expression architecture always seems poised on the verge of speech, as if buildings were about to start a conversation with humans. From this perspective, and contrary to what the strongly symbolic character of other visual arts might lead us to believe, architecture arguably bears a closer affinity to discourse. Over and against the pictorial or sculptural struggle to represent human scenes and actions, the very organization of architecture, its proportions and structure in particular, perforce suggests an abiding kinship with linguistic expression, and hence with the ideas and emotions formed by this organization.

At the same time, it is important to recognize that an edifice cannot be reduced to discourse. Matter always retains its share of obstinate silence, and to subjugate it entirely to the order of discursive reasoning is an unproductive, even dangerous, exercise. Some of the excesses of postmodernism—to which positions such as Reiser and Umemoto's are manifestly a reaction—bear witness to the failure of this sort of subjugation. In this respect, the famous cartoon published by Robert Venturi, Denise Scott Brown, and Steven Izenour in their 1972 manifesto *Learning from Las Vegas,* in which a building proudly holds up a massive billboard proclaiming "I am a monument," rings out like an alarm bell.[6] Even if the authors conceived of the image as a humorous plea to wrest architectural expression away from modernist codes (which they compared to a muzzle), and even if, to their minds, architecture should address the onlooker explicitly, the representation they devised has, in retrospect, garnered a somewhat different meaning. In the end, the declaration "I am a monument" is necessarily external to what gives architecture its substance; there is always a gap between the ordering of matter imposed by architecture and what an actual speech act implies.

Between architecture and language, one should probably consider that a perennial process of simultaneous convergence and distancing is actually taking place. Rather than favoring convergence over distancing, or the reverse, I would like here to scan the chronic incompleteness of the encounter between architecture and language in order to understand more fully the fundamental tension between the material opacity of architectural realization and its expressive will. There is no better illustration of this tension than the recurring frustration of architecture's desire to speak.

An understanding of the incomplete encounter between architecture and language may be further sharpened by an examination of one of the French philosopher Jacques Derrida's most influential volumes,

Language or the upper limit of architectural expression. Robert Venturi, Denise Scott Brown, and Steven Izenour, "Recommendation for a Monument," from *Learning from Las Vegas*, revised edition, page 156. Copyright 1977 Massachusetts Institute of Technology; reprinted by permission of The MIT Press.

De la grammatologie (Of Grammatology), first published in 1976. By means of his commentary on the works of the Enlightenment political philosopher Jean-Jacques Rousseau and the twentieth-century anthropologist Claude Lévi-Strauss, Derrida reveals how entire segments of Western intellectual thought have been infused by a desire for authenticity, which is often compared to seemingly spontaneous speech (as opposed to the artifice of writing).[7] He deconstructs this contrast between speech (a synonym for immediate presence) and writing (which necessarily refers to figures of distancing and absence, since the reader is not in the actual presence of the author) and undertakes to highlight the elements of mediation and absence that always remain embedded within speech, even in its most impromptu condition. By the same token, Derrida's analysis introduces the operations of *différance*—the differences and deferrals of meaning that undermine any pretense of real presence. Instead of assuming that the oral precedes the written, one must concede that something of the order of writing is already at work within speech itself, as a precondition for it.

The specter of real presence has always haunted the arts (despite the contemporary sense that such presence has been so diminished that its hold on the viewer is metaphysical and no longer totemic). This seems especially true of architecture, which offers to make matter expressive so that it seems about to speak. Yet in practice this speech act proves impossible precisely because architecture's effects are at the same time based on the obstinate silence of things and objects, which can be equated to distance or even to absence (following Derrida). To take this further, if there is something specious or inauthentic about the notion that architecture seeks to speak as humans do, this betrays what architecture owes to the opacity of matter. The insurmountable contrast between the spoken word (as a synonym of presence) and the written word (as a figure of absence) seems to find an equivalent in the discipline of architecture, which reveals a deeper ambiguity in its profound inclination toward language than other art forms for which authenticity coincides with orality. The presence of architectural creations seems indisputable, yet a certain type of absence remains secretly at work within them.

In this context, it is easier to understand the complicity between architecture and writing. This complicity first emerged during the Italian Renaissance with the appearance of treatises inspired by Vitruvius, and it still endures today. The example of Rem Koolhaas—author of *Delirious New York* (1978) and *S,M,L,XL* (1995), two of the most impactful architecture books of the late twentieth century—bears witness to the level of prestige attached to the architect capable of articulating ideas in writing; this lineage includes, among many others, Le Corbusier, Robert Venturi, and Aldo Rossi.

Writing, which is at the very least as enticing as speaking, reveals how effects related to distance and absence are inherent in the relationship between architecture and language. The written word—whether a book, an article, or an essay—prevents architecture from being defined only by what is built. Even though material realization typically constitutes the goal and focus of architecture, the discipline to some extent eludes or exceeds materialization, in the sense that architecture likewise resides in reflections that are only partially embodied in buildings. In this respect, it is striking to note that none of Le Corbusier's buildings (with the possible exceptions of Villa La Roche and the Villa Savoye) perfectly illustrate his "Five Points of Modern Architecture." Conversely, written text is ultimately powerless to convey, exhaustively, the substance of architecture. Things will always hold out against the words that seek to delimit them. From Leon Battista Alberti to Giacomo Barozzi da Vignola, the authors of Renaissance treatises never managed wholly to capture the subtleties of the new architecture inspired by antiquity, which they nonetheless sought to theorize in its most minute details. This dual gap—rendering the building ultimately inaccessible to the text and the text inaccessible to the building—has created a situation in which architecture is embodied by specific objects yet escapes encapsulation by these same objects, in which practice is bound by principles yet manipulates its dictates. This dual gap also means architecture can be both local and delocalized, both specific and generic. Either way, distancing and absence emerge as constitutive of architecture, as does the quality of indubitable presence.

Let us return to the architectural statement "I am a monument." What is a monument, other than that which, in the etymological sense, stands before us as a reminder of a person who is no longer there or of a past event? It is well known that monument and memory are intrinsically linked.[8] At the dawn of the Industrial Revolution, the romantics had a particularly keen awareness of the relationship between the two; in the chapter of his 1831 novel *Notre-Dame de Paris (The Hunchback of Notre Dame)* that he dedicated to architecture, Victor Hugo felt justified in comparing the monuments of the past with books written for the people:

> If the reader will now review what we have hitherto briefly, very briefly, indicated, omitting countless proofs and also a thousand objections, we are led to this conclusion: that architecture up to the fifteenth century was the principal register of humanity; that during this period, not a single thought of a complicated nature appeared in the world but was transformed into masonry; that all popular ideas as well as all religious law had their monuments.[9]

Reiterated here is how the bond of monument and memory, the opportunity to inscribe in stone that which is remembered, is a matter of the relationship with writing. In *De l'art en Allemagne* (published some ten years after Hugo's novel), the journalist, historian, and politician Hippolyte Fortoul went as far as to declare that "writing is the true architecture of the people."[10] Like the poet reciting verse, architecture seeks to speak to us of those who are no more, or of that which occurred long ago. Yet the words it formulates are inexorably transformed into traces; poetic spirit dries up as rules emerge that are similar to those that govern written expression.

To underscore the obvious, then, architecture is not made to match writing any more than it truly speaks. Hugo was in my opinion wrong in assuming that Gothic cathedrals operated like books for the public at large (I will return to this point in the last section of my Conclusion). The process of putting matter into order that architecture initiates is not reducible to what a rigorous system of syntax and vocabulary entails; if it were, architecture would succumb to a dull repetition of stereotypical sequences. It is in this sense that the "speaking architecture" of the last decades of the eighteenth century truly expressed itself, upstream from speech and downstream from writing. As Boullée theorized in *Essai sur l'art (Essay on Art)*, written in the 1780s, it is a matter of the discipline positioning itself prior to language by means of a geometry that establishes an analogy between elementary volumes—cube, sphere, cylinder, and pyramid—and primary human sensations as well as investing in symbols that presuppose the invention of writing in order to propagate myths and stories. The famous façade that Boullée designed as part of his project for the King's Library illustrates this double domain:

on the one hand, it features a parallelepiped volume summoning up perceptual codes that are supposedly more ancient than the invention of the spoken word; on the other hand, the doorway is adorned with a pair of Atlas figures bearing a vast globe. The latter motif is incomprehensible without an antiquarian—and so bookish—familiarity with the requisite myth.[11]

In sum, architecture's ambiguous relationship to language—and, more specifically (as exemplified by Boullée), its incomplete transition toward speech that morphs into a physical trace that, while ordered, never attains the syntactical rigor of discourse—is symptomatic of a broader attitude toward the problem of architectural expression: not enough expression, and we risk straying from architecture as such (Le Corbusier's Dom-Ino system deliberately toys with this condition); too much expression, and the architectural status of a given work is called into question. It is in this latter sense that Frank Gehry is often criticized for a mode of unrestrained gesticulation far removed from the sobriety

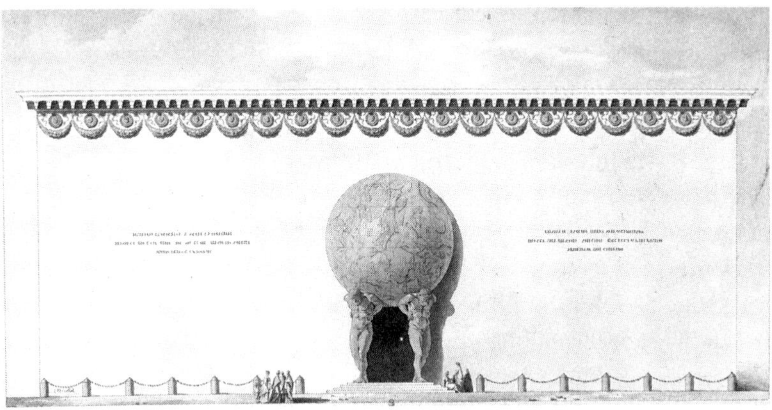

Étienne-Louis Boullée, project for the façade of the King's Library in Paris, 1788. Bibliothèque Nationale de France. A striking example of late eighteenth-century "speaking architecture": the project speaks prior to language through its massive rectangular volume and after language through its elaborate decoration. The inscriptions on both sides of the door mark the moment where language and architecture (or, to be more accurate, writing and architecture) coincide for a brief moment.

to which architecture is expected to adhere. Meanwhile, Ludwig Mies van der Rohe's output, inspired by the famous maxim "Less is more," remains one of the most accomplished examples of such sobriety; Mies's minimalism is far closer to what constitutes the core of the architectural discipline than any number of showy formal experiments.

Indeed, opting for expressivity means endeavoring to eliminate the distance separating architecture from speech—and deployment of the term *gesticulation* (in this case in reference to Gehry) underscores that gesture intends to be expressive. There is a history here. The very notion of "architectural gesture" so frequently evoked by critics today conjures up the "language of action" to which a number of Enlightenment commentators—from William Warburton, bishop of Gloucester, to the sensationalist philosopher Étienne Bonnot de Condillac—alluded. They associated the "language of action" with expressive bodily movements and so cast it as the immediate predecessor of speech. Hence the appearance of body motion suggested by the notion of "architectural gesture" can prove perilously close to speech and, consequently, to the loss of authenticity that affects an architecture that truly "speaks."

By the same token, the temptation to write is just as dangerous and flawed when it leads to a reliance on stereotypical vocabulary, motifs, and compositions. Over the course of the first decades of the nineteenth century, neoclassical architecture often fell into this trap; it invaded Europe as a truly "international style," relying as it did on essentially identical models from one country to the next (from Spain to Russia via France and Denmark). Willingly inspired by this kind of duplication more than 150 years later, the postmodernist movement did not escape its fate; precisely the same impression of disembodied stiffness runs throughout the compositions of the architectural pedagogue Jean-Nicolas-Louis Durand and the work of brothers Rob and Léon Krier, proponents of the New Urbanism. In both cases, the earnest search for expressiveness and the utter absence of expression strangely seem to converge, as if the spoken and written word had become indistinguishable from one another. Is it mere accident that the neoclassical period was one of the first to attempt the production of ornamentation on an industrial scale? The vases, medallions, friezes, and caryatids it rendered ubiquitous seem a fitting prelude to the advent of an architecture reliant on the assembly of prefabricated elements.

Prior to its condemnation by modernists and eventual rehabilitation by postmodernists, ornament had served as a reliable register of the tension between the alternating lack and abundance of expression running throughout architecture's history.[12] Ornament is, in the end, inseparable from the question of expression, right down to the linguistic connotations for which it has in various historical moments served as vehicle. The architectural speech act that was sought out at the end of the eighteenth century was, for instance, unveiled in ornamentation that corresponded to the intended effect; hence Boullée drew on highly symbolic decorative sources for the imagining of his most emblematic projects.

It is significant that one of the most venerable means of making manifest the expressiveness that ornament can bestow on buildings consists in superimposing the human face on molding profiles—as if the conjuring of an ideal physiognomy can inject a human appearance and capacity into architectural structures. This conviction is present, for example, in the first printed text published in Spanish, Diego de Sagredo's 1526 treatise *Medidas del Romano (The Measurements of the Romans)*. The physiognomic imperative later reappeared in Gian Lorenzo Bernini's writings and drawings as well as in the lessons devised by the eighteenth-century architectural pedagogue Jacques-François Blondel, who sought to showcase the spirit of the ornamental systems proposed by Andrea Palladio, Vincenzo Scamozzi, and Vignola.[13]

If the traditional deployment of ornament implies that a building is on the verge of speech, the repression of ornament, or its excessive standardization, causes architectural character to recede like the ocean's ebb. By the same token, decorative overabundance can compromise the architectural value of construction; to use another maritime metaphor, ornamental excess risks dulling the pure lines of an edifice just as marine deposits, shells, corals, and sponges gradually coat the hull of a sunken ship to the point of rendering it unrecognizable. There are baroque buildings, such as the Basilica of Santa Croce in the southern Italian city of Lecce, that bring to mind this process of covering and distorting through successive incrustations. This is clearly the strategy

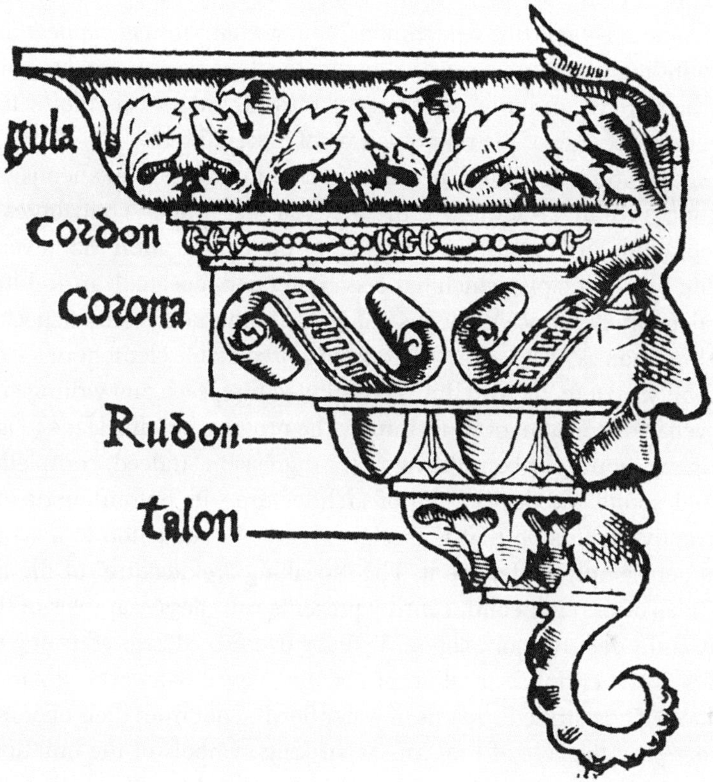

Diego de Sagredo, profiles of moldings with human head, from *Las medidas del Romano (The Measurements of the Romans)*, 1526. To ornament a building is to signify that it is on the verge of speaking.

pursued by Giovanni Battista Piranesi, whose entire project may be anachronistically interpreted as a radical alternative to Le Corbusier's Dom-Ino system. Whereas the former willfully tested the limits at which ornament might dissolve architecture's integrity, the latter approached the symmetrical limit of a radical disappearance of any form of décor. The profusion of decoration evidenced in Piranesi's *Parere su l'architettura (Opinions on Architecture)* (1765) relates to an advanced, indeed radically precocious, stage of architecture's transition to speech.[14] Here, ornament extricates itself from matter so as to become a purely symbolic system—and this detachment, which might initially appear as a resounding liberation from the obstinate silence of matter, backfires on the primary ambition to assert the meaningfulness of architecture precisely because of the relinquishing of materiality.

Architectural ornament must remain committed simultaneously to matter, or more accurately to the material that it often contributes to celebrating, and to the guiding lines of the composition that gives it order. This principle, which has been reiterated repeatedly in architectural theory ever since Vitruvius, safeguards ornament from unchecked proliferation as well as from becoming a predictable element in a fixed vocabulary. Here, the two limits constituted by speech and writing crop up yet again; ornament must initiate the progression that leads to language without ever completing that progression. Indeed, completion would sound the death knell of architecture—its entombment in a decorative profusion that is foreign to it, or its reduction to a syntax that serves only to deplete it. The "speaking architecture" of the last decades of the eighteenth century presents countless examples of this constantly deferred completion. Take the overturned urns adorning the walls of the entrance pavilion of Ledoux's Royal Saltworks at Arc-et-Senans. The petrified streams of water flowing out from their openings underscore the role of the urns as striking symbols of the building's vocation. Yet these urns retain an element of mystery, for their rustic profiles barely project out from the masonry—as if they were natural deposits accumulating on the stone surface.

Perhaps the most striking illustration of the necessity of incompletion lies in the contrast between the importance traditionally accorded to the Ionic order (one of the most frequently used in architecture) and the relatively marginal status of the caryatid. As it achieved its final transformation into a female body—a transformation initiated by the Ionic column—the caryatid came to lose much of its driving potential. It became too explicitly symbolic, and so could be used only on rare occasions as a sort of decorative apotheosis that exposed itself to pointless chatter. The fact that caryatids were serialized during the neoclassical period is symptomatic of the connection that can be made between,

Giovanni Battista Piranesi, imaginary architectural composition from *Parere su l'architettura (Opinions on Architecture)*, 1765. The ornamental proliferation threatens the very existence of an architectural order.

on the one hand, the temptation of chitchat and, on the other, the seduction of standardized writing; during the 1830s, one business based near Toulouse in southwestern France manufactured caryatids on an almost industrial scale.[15]

The condemnation of ornament that came in the wake of the Viennese architect Adolf Loos's famous essay *Ornament und Verbrechen (Ornament and Crime)* (1908) did not instigate any fundamental change to the complex relationship between architecture and language.[16] Modernism remained haunted by the question, and Bruno Zevi's injunction to structure modern architecture as a language was not the first expression of this recurring concern. Architecture turns toward language without ever eliminating the gap that separates the two. While the desire for expression helps to make architecture a reality, this same reality is extinguished by overly close proximity to words and speech, which attract it, like a moth to a flame, to an inaccessible and blinding sun. One can propose that architecture searches out expressive potency all the while avoiding an excess of effects and symbols that might compromise its vitally material essence. This tension between the opaque stability of matter and the revelatory light of language remains more present than ever.

A superficial interpretation of the contemporary architectural scene might suggest the reverse impression, however. Reiser and Umemoto's "asignifying signs" and Moussavi and Kubo's antisymbolic stance seem to imply that the relation to language is no longer featured in the designers' agenda. Again, the rejection of postmodernism plays a role in this attitude. But how not to be struck at the same time by the multiplication of formal gestures that has accompanied the rise of the "starchitects," from Frank Gehry to Zaha Hadid, and from Norman Foster to Herzog & de Meuron, to name only a few? Furthered by digital tools, which enable designers to manipulate complex geometries, these formal gestures evoke an early twenty-first-century version of the "language of action," as if the architectural discipline is returning to the ambition of the late eighteenth-century "speaking architecture" to express itself prior to language. What seems to be missing is the project to speak simultaneously after language, using a symbolic repertoire that presupposes its invention. The proponents of the "return" of ornament that is discussed extensively today claim to be devoid of any symbolic intention.[17] One may nevertheless wonder whether such a position is sustainable. Is it possible to deploy ornament with the innocence of an allegedly prelinguistic state of mind? The age of "asignifying signs" is in fact marked by the proliferation of texts and symbols; the Internet and its social media sites are brimming with them. Language and meaning have not disappeared—far from it—and it seems highly improbable that architecture can escape their entreaties for very long.

From a similar perspective, the "material turn" also appears to be an ambiguous enterprise. While it aims to break with the logocentric tradition of the West, it seeks to let objects speak, thus reconnecting with an intuition that the German philosopher Johann Gottlieb Fichte theorized in order to overcome the Kantian distinction between noumena and phenomena (objects in themselves and objects as they appear to us)—namely, that the very thought of an object presupposes a call or a summons of the object to the thinker.[18] In other words, in order to be recognized properly, objects must be able to address humans. Thus, just like contemporary architecture, the material turn seems unable to escape the question of language and its extension to the nonhuman realm. How is it that things are both mute and constantly on the verge of talking, from buildings to the objects studied by anthropologists and sociologists? In this expanded field of potentially talkative things, the specificity of the architectural discipline could very well reside in the intensity of architecture's longing for expression as well as in its refusal to let its productions truly speak. For architects, as much as it represents a constraint, the inscrutability of matter appears to be a dimension of good design.

3

Animation and Materiality

It seems important at this juncture to address the animation of matter, for this is a concept that helps us to reflect on the discipline of architecture, to frame the question of its expressivity, and to attain a better understanding of the ways in which language intervenes in the search for architectural expression. Above all, it provides an essential transition toward the detailed study of materiality and its role in architecture. The concept has ancient roots: for example, the Greek myth of Orpheus describes how the beautiful sounds emanating from his golden lyre caused trees and rocks to move and rivers to change their course; there is also Sextus Propertius's elegiac reference to the "lyre-built walls" of Amphion, son of Zeus and Antiope, whose melodies prompted boulders to stack themselves up to form the colossal walls of Thebes.[1] Although, as we have seen, architecture frustratingly never quite matches up with language, it arguably has a far more serene and easy relation to music—undoubtedly because both affect the body as well as the mind. This relation has fueled significant investigations into the intersections of harmony, proportion, resonance, and temperament (from Andrea Palladio's symphonic system of proportion to Peter Zumthor's Sound Box).[2]

Before embarking on a more detailed account of the kind of animation that architecture aims for, it is worth pondering the substance of a concept to which one typically refers without great thought, as if it

Amphion plays the lyre to build the wall of Thebes, after Antoine Caron, around 1615. Bibliothèque Nationale de France. An extreme case of architectural animation: the traditional analogy between architecture and music reveals the enduring character of the idea of architectural animation.

were self-evident. In truth, animation raises all sorts of questions, but what is certain is that it always pertains to matter—matter that can be animated in various ways. In the book of Genesis, God literally animates matter by creating Adam, the first man, from the dust of the earth. The English verb *to animate* stems from the Latin *animare,* which means to give life and is itself a derivation of *anima*—breath or life. God gives life to his creation by breathing into Adam's nostrils, and so to animate something is to breathe life into it. Likewise, nature has the power to animate, as is borne out by the various manifestations of organic life. This capacity was long interpreted as a sort of delegation of divine power, but from the materialist's perspective, it is nature, and nature alone, that gives life through the animation of matter.

The historical transition between a theologically dominated intellectual tradition existing since the Middle Ages and the secularized models of thought that coincided with the development of modern science in the seventeenth century is marked by, among other things, the philosophy of René Descartes.[3] Descartes set out to formulate a compromise between the two versions of *animare* haunting his intellectual world by speculating that God had set into swirling motion the undifferentiated matter of the universe—and so the world as we know it, with its stars, planets, and animated beings, is a result of this initial turmoil. However, Descartes drew a distinction in such writings as *Discours de la méthode (Discourse on Method)* (1637) between life in general—in other words, the animation incited by nature following the original movement communicated by God—and the life that characterizes humankind because it bears the mark of a conscious, rational mind. For Descartes, the animation of animals was of a different order than that of humans; the former remained merely mechanistic, akin to the activation of machines, while the latter entailed the creation of an immaterial soul endowed by God. As a pioneer of modern science and philosophy, Descartes was fascinated by the techniques and technologies developed in his time, along with the prospect of progress they represented. Since, in his eyes, there was no fundamental difference between animals and machines, this tended to prove that human beings must necessarily possess a certain power of animation; yet this power remains incomplete because it is impossible to endow one's own creations with a soul.

Descartes is by no means the only thinker to contrast full-fledged animation with the necessarily incomplete animation wrought by human hands. This theme, as ancient as it is modern, courses through religious doctrine, philosophical thought, and our most ambitious scientific and technological aspirations. Myth, fairy tales, science fiction—all have contributed to a vast opus on animation: from the Golem of Prague, the artificial anthropomorphic being made of clay by a late sixteenth-century rabbi, to the monstrous entity imagined by Mary Shelley in *Frankenstein; or, The Modern Prometheus* (1818); from the woman-machine described in the symbolist Auguste de Villiers de l'Isle-Adam's *L'Ève future (The Future Eve)* (1886) to the constantly "humming" mechanical hound in Ray Bradbury's *Fahrenheit 451* (1953). The imperfection of creatures that are generated by humans is an obligatory starting point in all of this. The plot thickens, however, when this initial imperfection is overcome, empowered even, and the creature really becomes alive, giving rise to all manner of catastrophes, exterminations, conflagrations, epidemics, and end-of-the-world scenarios.

By the same token, incomplete animation tends to be something that is quite specific to us. It is pride that ultimately drives humans to trespass, to cross the boundary—and the myth of the Titan Prometheus who steals the divine flame can be substituted for the story of the person who misappropriates from God or nature the life-giving spark, the flash of electricity, or the fragment of code. Despite these transgressions, incomplete animation remains one of the defining characteristics of the human condition, which is perceived and experienced as fundamentally limited. Hence, complete animation arouses fascination and anxiety, just as infinity inspires giddiness and fear. In the past, inventors of machines were often accused of sorcery, and their descendants provoke just as much disquiet. When a scientist of Stephen Hawking's caliber expressed deep concern over the development of artificial intelligence, which he considered to be the most serious threat ever to face humanity, he joined a long tradition of guardedness against a Promethean attitude that risks unleashing total cataclysm.[4]

From Shelley's *Frankenstein* to contemporary fiction on artificial intelligence, such as the 2015 film *Ex Machina,* it is significant that the capacity for linguistic expression constitutes one of the clearest signs that a boundary has been transgressed. This transgression jeopardizes the fragile balance that allows us to thrive, for speaking and writing inexorably belong to the human domain. A space of existential crisis is opened up when another kind of entity takes hold of linguistic communication.

In a probing essay, the French philosopher Pierre Caye has shown how the rise of humanism in architecture, as it appeared in the writings of Alberti and of Palladio's mentor, Daniele Barbaro, consisted in mobilizing the discipline so as to shield the mind from two equally formidable forces threatening the exercise of reason: divinity, or absolute transcendence, and nature, or immanence in its most accomplished form.[5] Architectural construction, in this scheme of things, allows for the establishment of an intermediate dominion between God and nature—that is, an arena in which human actions are privileged and thus acquire great significance. Another way to view the founding project of humanism, then, is to imagine architecture as forever creating the stage of a theater, the simple existence of which guarantees that our gestures and, above all, our words have a meaning that can be shared. Even when the lights are off and the audience is gone, the stage remains a magnet, attracting anyone who has wandered into the theater by chance; the simple act of having climbed the few steps that separate it from the rest of the space, of having crossed the proscenium or emerged from the wings, confers a special dignity to the person standing up there, on the stage.

Theatrical stages typically have scenery. In previous work on the subject of architectural ornament, I found myself referring back to Caye's interpretation of humanism in order to understand what, for example, a scholar like Oleg Grabar might have meant when he stated that architecture has no purpose other than to "adorn" our various activities.[6] My point here is that while the architectural animation of matter has typically found expression in ornament and décor (this is architecture's scenery, as it were), such animation has altogether more ambitious aims: to establish a world that is simultaneously related to and distinct from both the dwelling place of the gods and the natural kingdom. This is a world that allows human life to unfold meaningfully. This is the whole point of Vitruvian proportion and more generally of every traditional system of measurements that allowed buildings to be inhabitable.

However, in order for the unfolding to happen—for the setting of what Alberti called the human *historia* to be real to humans—matter needs to be animated; it needs to reach out to us, women and men, but without speaking. Put another way, the architectural animation of matter must necessarily remain incomplete, unfinished. This incompletion is what defines the world we create. Furthermore, incompletion is only seemingly a flaw, for in fact it functions as a sort of retreat or withdrawal that authorizes the actions and words of an unequivocally human kingdom to appear—this by means of a process reminiscent of the *tsimtsum* in the Kabbalah: the operation in which God contracted his light to allow a conceptual space for the true act of creation, which enabled the existence of a finite and independent reality beyond or outside the divinity.[7]

By contrast, complete animation, whether natural or divine in origin, does not allow humans to develop fully. Clearly, there are questions to be asked about the relevance of this traditional limitation today, in a time of unprecedented genetic manipulations and developments in artificial intelligence: How might these technological adventures and acquisitions alter the human reflex to retreat from complete animation? Questions such as this are likely to be posed, in particular, by those designing interactive environments.[8] Whether to limit animation or not remains, however, a fundamental issue for contemporary architecture.

Where architecture is concerned, animating matter means reaching out to human beings. It is not enough for building materials to give the appearance of being enlivened—for stone to be fashioned into foliage or for concrete to enact flexible curvatures in the manner of a cat's movements. The breathtaking art nouveau of Antoni Gaudí, Hector Guimard, and Victor Horta does not even come close to monopolizing the animation that is architecture's target. This goes much further than the branching structures, warped surfaces, and fibrous skeletons taken from the plant and animal kingdoms. Furthermore, it is not necessarily tied to mimicry. The overall movement of built masses generally appears to be a determining factor here. And in contemporary architecture, animation has once again called into play the search for forms of expression that evoke the potential relationship between humanity and matter. Connections and exchanges between humanity and matter must, in fact, be generated to ensure the emergence of that distinctly human domain that, because it belongs neither to the gods nor to nature, helps to constitute the human condition. The making of these connections and exchanges, then, lies at the heart of the architectural discipline, which explores them either by ordering matter (and thus fighting against its obstinacy) or by endeavoring to make it expressive (hence the turn to language). This dual enterprise goes hand in hand with the question of how matter influences consciousness and reason—how it conditions actions and shapes thoughts.

Antoni Gaudí, Casa Milà, Barcelona, 1910. The undulation of built masses, so vivid in Gaudí's projects, is not the only architectural means to animate matter.

The concept of the animation of matter does not solely concern our capacity as humans to identify with something outside ourselves (to the point of believing that we feel what that alien entity is feeling). We can, of course, project our very beings onto material objects—a capacity that architects and engineers often call up just as Torroja did when he demanded that structural designers internalize the principles of matter and movement "down to the very marrow of their bones."[9] But there are many other ways of explaining how matter influences who and what we are. In other words, the animation of matter has not only to do with identification and projection, a class of phenomena that constitutes the psychological basis for the notion of empathy (or *Einfühlung*) introduced by the late nineteenth-century German philosopher Robert Vischer to understand the effect that works of art have on the mind. Without seeking to deny the importance of this contribution, the psychology of art that was subsequently developed by art historians such as August Schmarsow and Heinrich Wölfflin is best placed in a broader perspective, within which material and intellectual dimensions beyond those normally addressed by art and architectural history prove critical.[10] Indeed, this is where *techne* rears its head—and one might argue that alongside artistic theories, materials, and works, machines play an essential role in the animation of matter. Their relevance cannot be reduced to the impression of familiarity with them that we often have. Valuable in this respect is the contribution of contemporary German media theory (or so-called media discourse analysis), which has paid close interest to recording devices such as the typewriter and the phonograph, and to filing systems, all the while circumventing the empathy they can arouse in their users.[11]

The point here is that the psychological, while crucial, is not the only dimension that affects the transition toward language initiated by architecture. This process cannot be reduced to the contrast between abstraction and empathy, which, for the German art historian Wilhelm Worringer (whose interests ranged from Gothic architecture to modern avant-gardes), was meant to expand the range of psychological mechanisms that underlie our consciousness of the connection between aesthetic forms and the civilizations that generate them.[12] In many cases, the erection of psychological bridges between the human mind and aesthetic forms is the product of perceptive codes and of a symbolic process based on complex layers of determination. Understanding this production requires us to move beyond the psychology of art so as to observe factors such as the range of techniques that are available in a given context. While integral to the interpretive framework, forms of knowledge and belief systems must be connected strictly to the material basis from which they unfold.

At this juncture, it is helpful to discuss in more details the concept of materiality, which, as noted earlier, is not the same as matter. On the one hand, to describe something as material—as opposed to something that might be termed immaterial—is to assert that we, humans, have a relationship with it that is based on a certain obviousness. The materiality of an object or phenomenon need not automatically translate into tangibility, like the stigmata of Jesus Christ touched by the apostle Thomas for proof of Jesus's resurrection. Rather, we should consider that what strikes us as material are those items whose existence seems to be woven into the fabric of things, independent from us, resisting our desires, and by the same token invested with some sort of inevitability (hence the opacity and obstinacy we are forced to confront).

On the other hand, asserting that an object or phenomenon possesses an immaterial character tends to deprive it of the obviousness of the physical objects around us, as do the actions of nature, whose principles seem totally independent of our existence and will. Consequently, the suspicion arises that the immaterial might well be nothing more than a product of our imagination. Are ghosts real? This question has been asked countless times and in radically different cultural contexts, including those shaped by the assumption that there is no distinction to be made between the natural and supernatural realms.

At first glance, materiality would seem to depend exclusively on an immediate experience of the world (so phenomenologists insist). This rootedness in concrete experience allows for material things and events to be separated from manifestations of a far more immaterial character. But by drawing a clear boundary between what falls immediately within the realm of the senses and what might well be a figment of the imagination, do we not risk revalorizing the age-old distinction between body and mind? From Plato to Descartes, the materiality of the body had long been set in opposition to the immateriality of the soul. Yet contemporary philosophy and neuroscience have forcefully called into question the hardened and arbitrary separation of body and mind—this Cartesian dualism, so called because it is in Descartes's writings that the concept found its most perfect articulation.[13]

In addition to the modern critique of Cartesian dualism, historians and anthropologists have proved far more sensitive to ways in which our bodies, perceptions, and sensations bear the indelible imprint of the society in which we live. We do not perceive the things around us independently from the contexts that shape us through childhood, adolescence, and adulthood; these are the contexts that filter the diversity of external stimuli and render them comprehensible. To quote the British art historian Michael Baxandall: "Living in a culture, growing up and learning to survive in it, involves us in a special perceptive training."[14] This training happens in close connection with the materials, tools, instruments, and machines that are at our disposal as well as with the social organization, the philosophical and religious concepts, and the artistic and scientific representations of the world that surround us—in a word, with the culture in which we are immersed.

Materiality has varied considerably over the centuries. Furthermore, the roster of phenomena and objects that are understood to be material has also undergone major changes. Between roughly 1840 and 1920, as Victorian spiritualism reached its peak, ghosts surely seemed more material than they do today, and their real presence was accordingly captured through all sorts of devices, from Ouija boards to turntables, and even through photography. The English paranormal investigator William Hope, leader of the Crewe Circle spiritualist group, capitalized on "spirit photography" by producing prints that were considered authentic by a clientele keen to communicate with the dead.[15] Today, the development of environmental attitudes toward buildings has meant that phenomena such as humidity and temperature gradients—in other words, variations in humidity and temperature instead of average values—are taking on a more tangible character than they did previously (a topic to which I will return).

It is worth emphasizing that materiality is likewise linked to the utilitarian materials of everyday life, beginning with construction materials. For instance, the pervasive presence of wood in early modern Europe had a lot of consequences for the way people related to the physical world. The machines and vernacular buildings that were made with it creaked, swelled, and molded with humidity and shrank when the weather was durably dry, thus evoking living beings reacting to their environment. In such a context, there was no clear-cut difference between natural objects and human-made ones. Unambiguous artificiality appeared as a hard-won achievement. Along these lines, the taste for artifice among preindustrial elites merits a whole study in itself. It is a fair bet that if Louis XIV had had access to plastics, Versailles would have made abundant use of them, starting with the Hall of Mirrors, that hymn to heterogeneity and artificiality with its glass, bronzes, canvases, and plasterwork.

The widespread employment of iron during the First Industrial Revolution marked an important turning point, and not only from a strictly technical perspective. By pervading whole areas of life, cast iron, wrought iron, and steel progressively plunged people into a world of objects whose precise contours modified their perception of the surrounding environment. Precision was not the only characteristic of the first industrial age; cast-iron decoration—firedogs, stoves, and apartment balconies—proliferated and became a prominent feature that made new aesthetic claims on space, and iron architecture itself made abundant use of ornamentation.[16] The adoption of reinforced concrete circa 1900 was another milestone, although in a more limited way, as it mainly affected civil engineering and construction. The spread of plastics in the aftermath of World War II was another major change that modified vastly different sectors of activity.

The use of materials is intimately related to our behavior in and perception of the tangible world. It reveals not only the existence of dominant patterns but also the presence of tensions and contradictions that mark the limits of these patterns—in other words, it contributes to the delineation of the regime of materiality that prevails at a certain moment in the evolution of a society. As I noted earlier, regimes of materiality, which encapsulate the characteristic features of a dominant approach to materiality, are built on points of consensus, but they also reflect unresolved issues. Because of these issues, one must exert caution when interpreting certain cases. If, for instance, one considers only the massive character of ancient Egyptian temples, one might draw overly simplistic conclusions regarding the conception of materiality underlying them. For a very long time, historians of architecture used large, monolithic stone as the perfect illustration of an ideal of sturdiness that predated the invention of the vault. Toward the end of the nineteenth century, the discovery that ancient Egyptians, using adobe instead of stone, had actually built lighter vaulted structures for utilitarian programs such as granaries and warehouses challenged this picture.[17] By the same

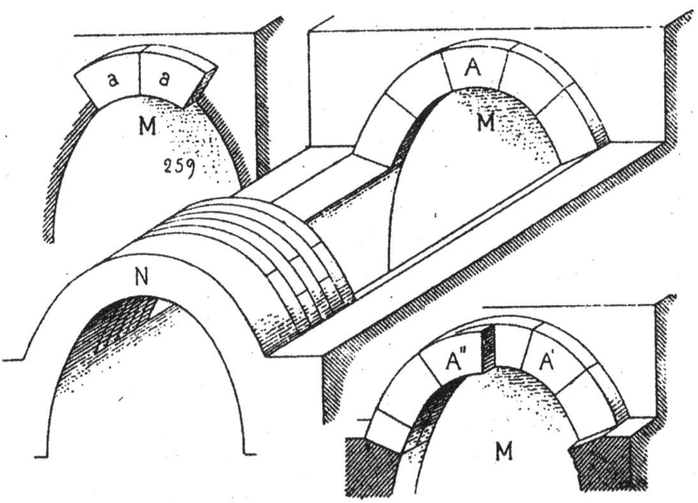

Ancient Egyptian barrel vaults in adobe, from Auguste Choisy, *Histoire de l'architecture (History of Architecture)*, 1899. Relations to materials often present striking contrasts. Nothing could be further from the massive stone temples of ancient Egypt than the light barrel vaults that covered utilitarian Egyptian buildings of the same period.

token, the relation of ancient Egypt to matter and materials began to appear far more complex than historians had initially envisaged.

A similar contrast exists today between the massive constructions, often blurring the distinction between buildings and infrastructure, that have been erected all over the United States, from giant office buildings to sports arenas, convention centers, and airport terminals, and the widespread use of light wood frames for suburban houses that seem to belong to a completely different universe. Home to both types of constructions, North America seems to pursue both heaviness and lightness, permanence and impermanence. The truth is that the relation to matter and materials is almost always complicated, and even contradictory, just like English art and architecture according to Erwin Panofsky, who interpreted them in the light of a recurring tension between classical rigor and romantic inspiration.[18]

This relation has become even more complex with the multiplication of new materials that has taken place in the past decades. On the one hand, humans have never invented so many of them; on the other hand, these materials generate uneasiness despite their extended properties, such as the capacity of structural glass to be both transparent and highly resistant.[19] With its plastics, composites, and smart materials, the present age is also an age of intense nostalgia for the lost authenticity of traditional materials. Unlike Louis XIV and his contemporaries, who saw artificiality in a mostly positive light, the women and men of the early twenty-first century often find it disturbing, even synonymous with a dystopian future. The current widespread attachment to stone chimneypieces and exposed beams represents a reassuring gloss on a vaguely identified past.

The use of materials is inseparable from techniques of assemblage, which contribute also to the relation between matter and humans. Think of the importance of carpentry joints in traditional Chinese and Japanese cultures. The importance of rivets in the perception of nineteenth-century iron construction, as well as their evocative power in the design of today's steampunk décors, constitutes another expression of the role played by techniques of assemblage in the relation between humans and their physical environment. Just like the attitude toward materials, the use of some of these techniques reveals profound contradictions in this relation. For instance, it is well known that the use of glue should be prohibited, or at least severely limited, for the sake of environmental sustainability. A sustainable product must be easy to disassemble, something that glue evidently prevents.[20] Despite the contemporary concern for the planet, glue is used on a massive scale, in everything from industrial products to buildings. Without it, composite materials, with their lighter weight and increased resistance, would not be possible.

The systems of proportions and the standards mobilized to order materials contribute as well to the constitution of regimes of materiality. These tools not only embody scientific and technological knowledge, such as the understanding of materials' resistance to compression, traction, and bending, but they also reflect the visual habits, tastes, and values of a given society, thus contributing to the "special perceptive training" that Baxandall invokes as one of the foundations of culture. While they do not tell us the complete story of the relation between ancient Egypt and its materials of construction, the massive proportions of ancient Egyptian temples are nevertheless emblematic of some key aspects of the Egyptians' attitude toward the physical world. Similarly revealing are the slenderness of Gothic proportions and their subsequent abandonment by the Renaissance in relation to the rise of a new regime of materiality.

Structural intuitions and practices are present in the formation of regimes of materiality. Together with techniques of assemblage and systems of proportions and standards, they reflect the way materials are experienced and understood in relation to cultural and social values. The Gothic system of light vaults, columns, and abutments has been often connected to various medieval aspirations, from the hubris of the princes and bishops who sponsored the construction of large churches to the shared faith of the people who actually built them.[21] Starting with the 1851 Crystal Palace, the builders of the great nineteenth-century exhibition halls aimed to promote a collective belief in the material and spiritual progress of humankind, and thus designed their halls to appear as the cathedrals of the industrial age.[22] Their use of iron and glass was closely linked to this project imbued with a utopian dimension. Similarly, the development of light structures throughout the twentieth century cannot be separated from a loosely defined but pervasive political and social agenda centered on the desire to free humanity from the unnecessary burdens of an industrial age now perceived as antiquated. In North America, Buckminster Fuller was among the key advocates of structural developments widely interpreted from a perspective of emancipation. The notion of "ephemeralization" that he introduced in his writings to characterize this overall approach to structural design, and more generally to technology, was not only about doing more with less material; it also implied a profound redefinition of the relation of humanity to the resources of the planet and the lifestyle derived from it.[23]

Apart from materials and the practical and conceptual tools used to order them, such as proportions and structure, materiality depends crucially on instruments and machines, and these are often related to broad philosophical, aesthetic, and scientific concepts. When Galileo pointed a telescope toward the moon and discovered the craggy irregularities of its surface, he shattered an ancient representation of materiality that was founded on the contrast between a perfect and unchanging celestial universe and an earthly realm subject to the caprices of generation and corruption. The laws of mechanics, and especially the principle of inertia, could thereafter be applied to both the sublunar and the supralunar realms.[24]

Even more than scientific instruments, the machines that shape the technological environment—such as the steam engine in the nineteenth century and the automobile in the twentieth—are determining factors in the experience of materiality. Nothing is more revealing in this respect than the automobile. Its adoption changed not only people's perceptions of territorial and urban space but also their relationship with the human body. Subjected every day to accelerations and decelerations, bodies were simultaneously glorified (because of the mechanical strength and speed that made manifest fearsome power) and rendered tragically abject (by the accidents that crushed them instantly into terrifying formlessness). This vulnerability is one of the central themes

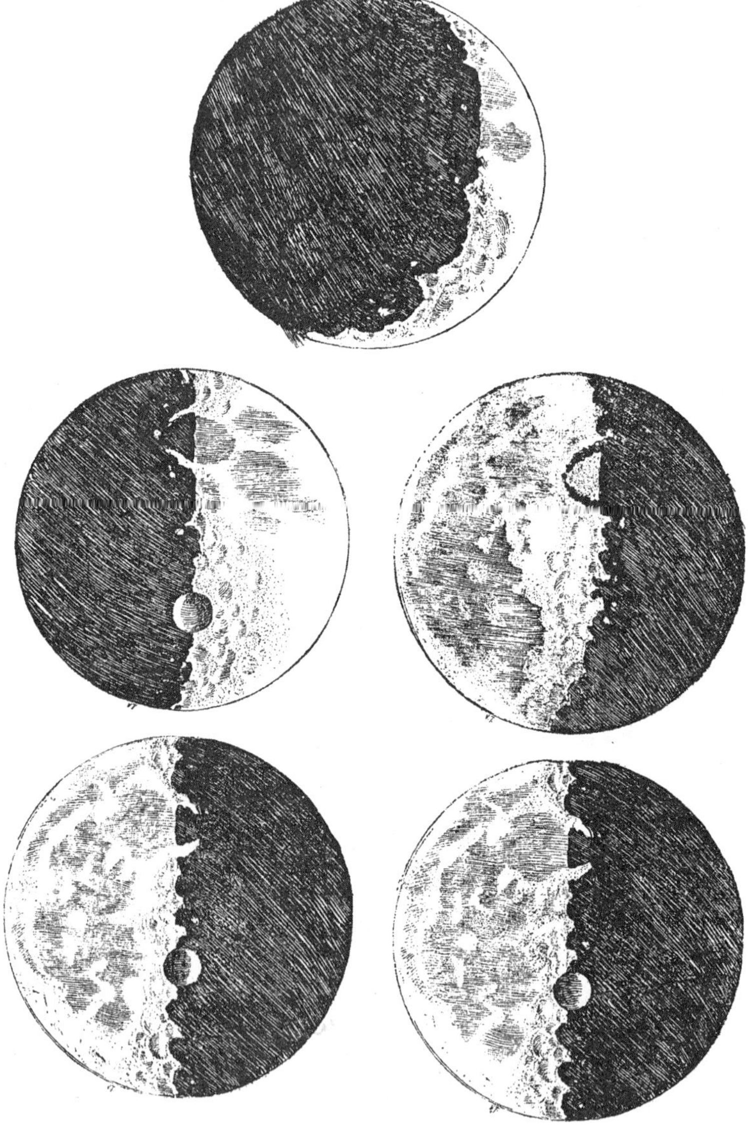

Galileo's sketches of the moon from *Sidereus nuncius*, 1610. Materiality depends on our scientific theories and instruments.

of James Graham Ballard's 1973 novel *Crash,* which portrays a community of people fascinated by car accidents and their effects on the human body.[25]

It is often assumed that machines are fundamentally different from humans. Clearly, the latter are not like automobiles. An abundant literature today insists on the difference between the way human beings think and the way computers use big data and algorithms. Deep learning differs profoundly from traditional learning. Simultaneously, we humans invent machines and relate to the physical world through them, as if some parts of our brains and bodies were mechanical. Two and a half centuries ago, long before the invention of the automobile or the computer, the French philosopher Denis Diderot, one of the editors of the *Encyclopédie,* was already asking himself to what extent humans were comparable to machines or at least better understood as somewhat analogous to them.[26] Through machines, materiality thus engages more than our relation to the physical world and the tangible objects and phenomena that populate it. It has to do with the very way we conceive ourselves. I will return to this issue shortly.

Deeply absorbed in plans to organize the relationship between matter and humanity, making abundant use of materials and their techniques of assemblage with the help of systems of proportionality and tectonic principles, architecture inevitably comes up against the question of materiality and of the objects and devices that most embody its evolution, beginning with the state-of-the-art machines that surround humans, often destabilizing them, while contributing to their understanding of themselves. No surprise, then, that starting with the Italian Futurists, modern architecture was quick to make the automobile into one of its fetish objects. "A roaring car that seems to ride on grapeshot is more beautiful than the Victory of Samothrace," was a brilliant proclamation of the 1909 Futurist Manifesto.[27] Noting that the automobile allowed people to move about twenty times faster than they could on foot, Le Corbusier insisted on the need to adapt modern urbanism and architecture to this new reality. "The secular milieu of simple speeds can no longer resist twentyfold speeds," he declared in a 1932 lecture in Barcelona.[28] But speed is only one of the myriad components that shaped humans' new relationships with a physical world shaken up by mechanical civilization and its most emblematic means of transport. It is in this context that the architectural use of materials such as concrete should be considered, as well as the return to elementary geometries; these aspects allowed architecture to appear as an anchor in environments beset by increased and dizzying mobility.

If the Villa Savoye occupies a key position in Le Corbusier's pre–World War II output, it is because the building is a particularly clear embodiment of these issues. It is not insignificant that the villa was designed to be reached by automobile—hence the garage under the pilotis. The mechanical journey up to the villa is followed by the architectural promenade leading from the ground floor to the main rooms only to terminate, after a series of slowdowns, at the solarium. It is as if the architecture, acting as a giant decelerator, has set out to reconcile

Maurice-Louis Branger, Grand Prix of Automobile Club de France, 1914. Copyright Maurice-Louis Branger/Roger Viollet. Few machines have had as great an impact on materiality as the automobile, which modernist architects and urban planners claimed as a major source of inspiration.

travel by car, and then by foot, with contemplative immobility. Direct contact with the machine and sensations aroused by speed give way to a calmer apprehension of architectural space, and then to the discovery of a natural order made simultaneously real and symbolic by the sunlight pouring in.[29]

Modernism was influenced by many other instruments, machines, and technologies. In a penetrating study, American historian Michael Osman has shown how American architecture in particular was influenced at the turn of the nineteenth century to the twentieth by the diffusion of the thermostat, which led to a renewed conception of the domestic interior as well as to the development of new types of facilities, such as cold storage.[30] The thermostat was part of the more general development of regulatory thinking that expanded the parameters with which architecture could play. Temperature and humidity were among the new dimensions that design could factor in, an evolution that clearly paved the way for the postwar rise of the ideal of the "well-tempered environment" discussed by Reyner Banham in his pathbreaking eponymous book, a rise that clearly corresponds to a turn in the history of the materiality of architecture.[31] Today, the consideration of gradients instead of average values may very well signal another turn, or rather a major inflection, in this history.

Moving beyond the scope of modernism, similar analyses could elucidate the links in different historical periods between architectural processes and materiality as bearing the mark of the materials, instruments, and machines affecting the physical world. Viewed in this way, the advent of the computer is emblematic of another profound transformation of materiality. Connected objects and the Internet of things could lead to another transformation of the relation between humans and the physical world through a different conception of animated things: being connected and exchanging information appearing as a new type of animation without equivalent in the past. From the sedan chair to the steam engine, from early modern automata to the robot, from thermostats to contemporary connected objects—the theme of the succession of technical devices and objects that have fascinated architects makes possible another kind of history of the discipline, one that is more wide-ranging in its assessment of materiality than a stricter focus on building materials and structural techniques allows.

To reiterate, materiality is not matter; rather, it is relational and so governs the relationship between humans and matter. Furthermore, materiality should not be understood merely as a representation of this relationship or as a collective mental image shared by members of a given culture. For one thing, it is fraught with tensions and contradictions, and as such is more akin to a field than to a unified conception, something like a paradigm. Above all, materiality involves the body as well as the perceptions and sensations that it incites. This corporeal dimension is inseparable from a series of practices, there again irreducible to shared mental images. Materiality is imperious, akin to a mode of being in the world that oversees the interaction between humans and all the objects and phenomena that are considered to be material. By means of materiality, matter ultimately becomes the opaque and resistant other of humanity. Opacity, however, is never absolute; it always leaves room for possible animation, which, perhaps, is precisely what architecture targets as its own. Humanity is partly defined through the confrontation with the opacity and obstinacy of matter, a confrontation that can just as easily result in an exchange, or rather a contagion—then things may become animated. Matter and humanity, obstinate silence and inquisitive subjectivity, engage in an endless pas de deux over the course of which the partners sometimes switch places. While humans seem to be leading the dance, objects and phenomena sometimes take over. Materiality, then, can also be interpreted as the ballet they create together. To put it in simpler terms, materiality contributes to the emergence of subjectivity as simultaneously opposed to and close to matter.

One of the most striking allegories of this dynamic complementarity between the constitution of the human self and the assertion of matter's opacity and resistance is found in the *Traité des sensations (Treatise on the Sensations)* (1754), by the Enlightenment sensationalist philosopher Étienne Bonnot de Condillac. Here, Condillac describes a statue endowed with intelligence but deprived of the senses. By successively investing the statue with smell, hearing, taste, sight, and finally touch, the philosopher evokes its gradual awakening to the world of sensations and ideas. Each sense incites its own set of discoveries, but the real tipping point is when the statue acquires the sense of touch. With touch, the statue discovers the existence of obstacles beyond itself; the external resistance of things coincides, of course, with the statue's realization that it possesses a body to interact with those things. The inertia and impenetrability of matter give access to true consciousness—an awareness of the self as an entity simultaneously linked to the world and distinct from it. Condillac's sentient statue is all the more interesting in that it does not presuppose a spontaneous empathy between humans and matter. In the purest Enlightenment tradition, their relationship appears more mechanical than psychological. It stems initially from collision rather than complicity, even if it subsequently produces a phenomenon of association between certain material configurations and certain mental states—a mechanism that allows an analogy to be made between these two categories.

Contemporary neuroscientists like Antonio Damasio seem at times to echo Condillac's conception of an organic bond between the unfolding of a person's subjectivity and the exploration of the physical world through the body.[32] Inspired by this hypothesis, historians such as Lynn Hunt have introduced the notion of "embodied self" to point toward the same connection between the constitution of subjectivity and the interaction of the body with the world.[33] The contemporary Japanese architect Tadao Ando, for his part, proposes a striking transposition of this intuition to architecture when he describes how the understanding of one's identity, the "I" that corresponds to one's body, is in his opinion inseparable from the perception of space and materials, a process that he calls the *shintai* and that could easily be related to what it means to truly inhabit a place, or to dwell, as Heidegger would have put it. For Ando, the *shintai* constitutes the true foundation of architecture, what makes it both possible and desirable:

> Man articulates the world through his body. Man is not a dualistic being in whom spirit and the flesh are essentially distinct, but a living corporeal being active in the world. . . .

> The body articulates the world. At the same time, the body is articulated by the world. When "I" perceive the concrete to be something cold and hard, "I" recognize the body as something warm and soft. In this way the body in its dynamic relationship with the world becomes the *shintai*. It is only the *shintai* in this sense that builds and understands architecture. The *shintai* is a sentient being that responds to the world.[34]

What Ando says of materials and their relation to the perception of the body applies equally to proportions and structure. As we have seen, both present strong connections with corporeal perception. In fact, most of the tools mobilized by architecture to order matter have links with the way humans, at a given moment, understand themselves, beginning with their bodies, to the point that the first question architects should probably ask themselves concerns the historically determined subject for whom they are designing and the type of body that person has. Designing for a Renaissance subject is not the same as designing for a contemporary cyborg-like individual.

But let us return to Condillac. Though it would be tempting to bring together the special status that he gives to the sense of touch and the strong interest taken in the tactile dimension by contemporary architecture under the influence of digital tools, the impact of his sensationalist philosophy on the architectural theory and practice of the second half of the eighteenth century is more telling. Following the sensationalist philosophy lesson, Nicolas Le Camus de Mézières set out to reflect on "the analogy of the proportions of architecture with our sensations," and Boullée took up this notion in *Essai sur l'art*.[35] By pondering matter, architecture came to be intimately associated with the awakening of consciousness and the development of mental faculties. For Enlightenment architects, the power that matter possessed to provoke sensations and ideas justified their discipline's pretensions to "speak." More generally, materiality raises questions about the connection between what falls within the realm of the senses and the language that serves to organize sensations and perceptions into conscious thoughts and emotions. Another way to define materiality, then, is to consider that it helps to articulate the boundary line—one that changes across different periods and societies—between silent objects and phenomena and things that can be said or written. Standing at the frontier between these two continents is architecture, which takes after both as it attempts to speak and to write, to utter and to inscribe, without ever surrendering its power to resist language.

Materiality contributes to construction at a much larger scale, once it is understood as engaged in the simultaneous emergence—or, more accurately, coproduction—of the radical nonhumanity of matter out of which things are made and a subjectivity that is conscious of what both unites it with and distinguishes it from what is exterior to it (what it is to be made of the same substance as things while at the same time experiencing their opacity and resistance). What emerges from this larger process of construction is nature, or rather the nonhuman realm, alongside the human domain. Materiality acts as a force within this process, which mobilizes all sorts of resources at a given time and in a given society. Like materiality, nature refers to the human ambition to stand apart from the world around us as well as to the awareness that we remain consubstantially united to it. Like materiality, nature refers more readily to the complex relationships erected between the human and the nonhuman than to the existence of a predetermined set of objects and phenomena that remain completely external to humanity.

In this regard, I find it difficult to share the astonishment of the French philosopher and sociologist of science and technology Bruno Latour, one of the founders of actor-network theory, when faced with a modernity that has both multiplied hybrids of human and nonhuman and attempted in some ontological sense to separate the two. Latour writes:

> The word "modern" designates two sets of entirely different practices which must remain distinct if they are to remain effective, but have recently begun to be confused. The first set of practices, by "translation," creates mixtures between entirely new types of beings, hybrids of nature and culture. The second, by "purification," creates two entirely distinct ontological zones: that of human beings on the one hand; that of non-humans on the other.[36]

Is this attitude so remarkable, at least in the Western tradition? Does it really belong only to the province of the "modern"? Can it truly be distinguished in this way from those periods that preceded it or will follow? Modernity may no longer be the dominant cultural frame, but it seems that we have not fully confronted the concrete implications of blurring the dividing line between human and nonhuman.

The modern attitude is, in some sense, a consequence of the curse that prevents humans from ever defining their identity without first referring to all of these things, these objects, that are set apart from them but are, paradoxically, part of what makes them who they are down to their very core. At the same time, they generally refuse to acknowledge the full consequences of the proximity between the human and the nonhuman. In this respect, there is nothing exceptional about modernity at all. At best, it can be considered paroxysmal in its need for "purification," to borrow Latour's expression—although it is likely the case that the moderns never completely believed in this possibility to begin with. After all, did they not advocate reengaging with nature by technological means (a theme to which I will return)? Even as we humans tirelessly, and with heroic effort, attempt to distance ourselves from what is around us—to escape the ties that bind us to the nonhuman—we know full well that the task is ultimately destined to fail, barring divine intervention or the summoning up of some sort of ontological difference that cannot possibly be based on objective factors. And yet the escape from such ties is imperative if we are to perpetuate the prospect of a specifically human destiny.

The always incomplete process of detachment would seem somewhat desperate if matter could not be animated, for even partial animation certifies the existence of that arena destined solely for humankind. In other words, the task of animation is to render impurity bearable. Within the human arena, the temptation to distinguish mind from matter remains strong (Descartes's dualism has never entirely given up the ghost). Yet this arena could not exist were it not for the ties that bind human beings to the things around them. In reality, mind is inseparable from matter, just as the human is inseparable from the nonhuman. This brings to mind the wonderful passage in which the philosopher of science François Dagognet comes to the defense of things and objects, long devalued in favor of ideas:

> The world of objects, which is immense, is in the end more revealing about the mind than the mind itself. In order to know what we are, it is not necessarily within ourselves that we should look. Philosophers throughout history have focused too exclusively on subjectivity, failing to comprehend that it is, to the contrary, in things that the mind can be most clearly seen. A true revolution is therefore needed, by realizing that it is far more within the realm of objects that the mind is to be found than within the realm of the subject.[37]

Precisely because it accords a central place to materiality—that is, to the simultaneous construction or coproduction of the material world and subjectivity—architecture blurs the boundary between making and expression. It gives order to matter and animates it, so that it can address human beings. More accurately, it speaks to us of a space in which our actions acquire meaning through contact with appropriately designed and arranged objects. Materials and their various techniques of assemblage, proportions, and structures, but also ornaments, have been enrolled in this project in different ways and at different moments in history. The role devoted to ornament in premodernist architecture is especially revealing in that respect. First, architectural ornament, which is usually interpreted from a mostly symbolic perspective, is in fact inseparable from the ordering of matter. The Latin word for ornament, *ornamentum,* shares a common etymological root with the verb *ordino,* meaning to organize, to order, a kinship that did not escape the Austrian-born British art historian Ernst Gombrich when he chose to call his masterly synthesis on ornamentation *The Sense of Order.*[38] Architectural ornament glorifies the harmonious layout of matter. Second, ornament has evidently to do with expression, thus reaffirming the strong link between making and addressing humans that characterizes the architectural discipline. Last, but certainly not least, this summoning is supposed to function at a collective level. Ornaments rely on the possibility of sharing meaning, hence the recurring temptation to interpret them as a sort of language. Beyond their use, in relation to language but always distinct from it, architecture makes the adventure of shared significance possible, a significance that stems from the experience of the tangible world. It is in this way, to return to Grabar, "that it is always at the service of man, and that it has no other purpose than to adorn his manifold activities."[39] Accessory though it may seem at first, this adornment enables humans to inhabit buildings and cities.

4

Architectural History and Regimes of Materiality

Materiality gives us a perspective on the history of architecture that is different from the one that generally prevails in textbooks. And while the potential reevaluation that materiality prompts does not necessarily call into question the main milestones of the field, it suggests new types of interpretation of key moments and contexts. In particular, it allows us to circumvent, and even perhaps to dispense with, the intractable opposition between traditional approaches that place emphasis on the intellectual and artistic dimensions of the discipline (including the ideals that it sets out for itself as well as the imagination, concepts, and models that guide architectural production) and more recent historiographical trends that consist in favoring those social and technical dimensions of design practices, which can be described through theoretical frameworks such as borrowings from media studies or actor-network theory.[1] Materiality can be reduced neither to a system of values and representations nor to a set of social relationships forged through physical devices and technical procedures. As seen earlier, materiality is fundamentally relational, meaning that it characterizes the encounter between things and objects that are meant to interface with the senses and the human beings who live in contact with those objects. Materiality, in short, simultaneously articulates the realm of values and representations and the realm of concrete practices. It appears as a complex field fraught with tensions and contradictions rather than as a totally coherent set of interconnected representations and practices.

The digital turn to which architecture has borne witness over the past two decades or so is frequently compared to the founding historical period of the discipline, namely, the Italian Renaissance.[2] Beyond superficial similarities, both of these periods were transitional, marked by changes in the relationship between humankind and the material world. There is little doubt that the Renaissance represented a profound transformation of this relationship. Think, for instance, of the Italian architectural historian Giulio Carlo Argan's account, in his analysis of Filippo Brunelleschi's invention of perspective, of the fifteenth-century turn to immanence and the material world.[3] As many authors have shown, the Renaissance saw the gradual superimposition of an ordered set of measurable spaces and objects onto the wondrous and suprareal world of the Middles Ages—a world populated by objects and creatures with extraordinary properties, a world that knew nothing of the laws of perspective. I use the term *superimposition* because monsters and wonders always remained lodged beneath the regularizing framework that Renaissance painters, sculptors, and architects cast across their worldly universe. Following the various authors who grappled with Vitruvian theory, this framework was like a net intended to render tangible the play of regular lines, surfaces, and volumes along with the proportional relationships that governed them. This spatial regularity pointed more generally at a world in which parts and wholes, but also causes and effects, were commensurate, thus opening the possibility of a new rational approach to problems.

While Michel Foucault, in *Les Mots et les choses: Une archéologie des sciences humaines (The Order of Things: An Archaeology of the Human Sciences)*, focused on the Renaissance play of likenesses and similitudes that continued to evoke the monsters and wonders inherited from the Middle Ages, the art historian Michael Baxandall favored instead the emergence of a different perspective on the physical world.[4] In *Painting and Experience in Fifteenth-Century Italy* (1972), he offered an admirable analysis of how, precisely, a new relationship with matter and materiality influenced Renaissance paintings commissioned by merchants accustomed to the visual evaluation of quantities, lengths, heights, surfaces, and volumes.[5] In this sense, art served as a particular expression of a much broader evolution, over the course of the 1400s, of the relationship with tangible things—a relationship that inexorably asserted its dependence on order and proportion founded on mensuration.

It was arguably architecture that was most marked by the transition to an ordered material world. Order meant that architecture could be confirmed as a creative and intellectual discipline with a canon of its own, including ancient Roman monuments and the selective roster of contemporary creations judged worthy of those of the classical period. Brunelleschi's dome for Florence Cathedral and Donato Bramante's Tempietto are part of this roster, and the high esteem in which they were held served to legitimate the larger ambition for spatial ordering, which was not limited to buildings. In Italy and subsequently in the rest of Europe, the regular compositions of the Renaissance architects began to transform urban environments. Indeed, the advent of an architecture openly inspired by the models of antiquity came about in close connection with the use of measuring devices and increasingly standardized practices such as mapping and surveying as well as with the impact of the new rational thought that was spreading throughout

Attributed to Fra Carnevale, *The Ideal City*, around 1480. Walters Art Museum, Baltimore, Maryland. This painting illustrates a double movement toward the spread of perspectival representation and the emergence of the city as a project. Both phenomena are linked to the Renaissance shift in the conception and experience of materiality.

the arts and sciences.[6] The lure of perspectival representation and the subsequent recourse to the orthographic sequence of plan, section, and elevation reflect this complicity.

Where construction techniques were concerned, Renaissance architecture gradually moved away from the boldness of Gothic buildings in favor of a self-imposed ideal of moderation. While the influence of the master builders of the Middle Ages remains palpable in the work of Brunelleschi in Italy and Philibert de l'Orme in France, the definitive break from a medieval past stemmed from a deliberate decision to create a convergence between the proportions derived from antiquity and technical prescriptions. Inspired by Vitruvius's writings, the premise of solidity to which practitioners and theorists referred rested precisely on this convergence.[7] In this new framework, Gothic buildings appeared too febrile and soaring, and their flamboyance went against both common sense and good taste.

Curbing the late medieval tendency toward virtuosity in the applied arts and architecture was a corollary to the new importance given to antiquity.[8] It accompanied the rise of design, understood as a conceptual production rather than as the mastery of a series of skills. This shift also involved the change in attitude toward matter and materials evoked above. The brilliance of the craftsman overcoming the various difficulties that arose when one tried to enroll materials in highly complex schemes was supposed to be superseded by the calm genius of the architect and artist, who mastered such schemes from above, using order and proportion. Of course, skills remained essential in painting and sculpture, but their role was greatly diminished. As for architecture, the abandonment of Flamboyant compositions and décors entailed a more radical break from the ideal of virtuosity, even if this change was in fact gradual in countries like England and France.

The birth of architecture as a discipline coincided with the invention of modern fortification and the development of urban mapping, which were equally premised on a world of regular and measurable things.[9] Take Leon Battista Alberti, who was not only one of the most prominent architectural theorists of his time but also one of the pioneers of urban mapping; his *Descriptio urbis Romae (Description of the*

City of Rome), a short text written in the 1440s, describes a representational method based on this fundamental assumption regarding the physical world.[10] This kind of rationalism was deployed not just for architecture but, more broadly, for the city. The bastion fortification system—created by Italian architects and engineers and then perfected by their French counterparts (from Francesco di Giorgio Martini and Vincenzo Scamozzi to Jean Errard de Bar-le-Duc to Sébastien Le Prestre de Vauban)—is inseparable from this hypothesis, with the dimensions of component parts dictated by firing lines and ranges.[11] Measuring distances and aiming from afar were fundamental to the triangulations on which Renaissance city plans were based.[12] At the intersection of mapping and modern fortification, the city as a whole began to appear as something that could be designed, an evolution illustrated by the rise of the theme of the ideal city, a city systematically fortified, from Filarete's utopian project Sforzinda, conceived sometime around 1464, to the planning and construction of Palmanova from 1593 onward.

It is important at this juncture to underscore the strong links between the changing attitudes toward the material world that unfolded over the course of the fifteenth and sixteenth centuries and the emergence of a new conception of the human that formed the basis of Renaissance humanism. Anthropomorphism was a key feature of this conception. It positioned the ideal human body as the measure of everything. Perspectival representation refers to the ordering power of the human gaze. In an enlightening essay, the Belgian historian Carl Havelange ties the wholly emblematic status that perspective enjoyed in this respect to the recalibration of the connection between the spectator's eye and the world.[13] The Renaissance monocular gaze tended to extract itself from the physical world, contrary to the medieval conception of vision, which posited that the eye was immersed in and not separable from the world. This new conception enabled the gaze to form a reasonable image of what lay before the viewer by means of a schema that was founded on measurement. Perspective is a product of this act of withdrawal, which fashions a plane between the observer and the world, a plane on which is inscribed the projection of the objects that fall within the purview of vision—hence, the birth of the perspectival view. Perspective, which prefigures the orthographic sequence, likewise refers to the measurable character of the world, but in a particular way: by bringing the world back to the visual experience of a single subject who is able to grasp distances and scale.

Similarly, the status that came to be attached to Vitruvian proportions over the course of the fifteenth and sixteenth centuries is inextricably tied to a reinterpretation of the connections between macrocosm and microcosm, between the universe and the individual subject, precisely because, as we have seen, these extremes were understood as flowing from one to the other. Renaissance architecture, then, is the definitive expression of the simultaneous reformulation of the subject's relation to the material world and the enshrinement of the human gaze in the perspectival mechanism that refers to the emergence of humanism. The full impact of the rupture between Gothic construction and this approach to architecture, enriched as it is with references to antiquity, is comprehensible only when placed within the broader context of the transformation of materiality understood as the relation between matter and humans.

The second half of the eighteenth century takes us to another turning point in the conception of materiality. This is the period that inaugurates, for the Viennese art historian Emil Kaufmann, the onset of architectural modernism—hence the provocation in the title of his well-known book *Von Ledoux bis Le Corbusier (From Ledoux to Le Corbusier)* (1933), which broadcasts the argument that Claude-Nicolas Ledoux's formal innovations were, in fact, anticipations of the designs of the architect of the Villa Savoye.[14] Following from Kaufmann, numerous studies have treated the theoretical and practical shifts that architecture underwent in relation to the Vitruvian tradition.[15] Many interpret this shift to be a consequence of the social and political philosophies of the decades leading up to and including the French Revolution.[16] Less common, however, are attempts to set architecture after 1750—and the evolution of ideas, forms, and programs it fueled—against a concomitant transformation of assessments of the physical world. Yet important examples—such as the influence of the French philosopher Étienne Bonnot de Condillac's 1754 work *Traité des sensations* on so-called visionary architects like Boullée and Ledoux, and the terms of heated debate between architects and engineers over the principle of architectural solidity—should encourage us to investigate Enlightenment conceptions of materiality somewhat more carefully.[17] As historian of architecture Erika Naginski observes, there was in this period a "general shift away from seventeenth-century understandings of matter as essentially passive and subject to God's arbitrary judgment. The presumed dependence of material bodies on external forces was a premise that sat squarely at the center of baroque theological doctrine, political philosophy, and scientific thought. . . . By contrast, the Enlightenment gradually sought out a markedly less-deterministic position. It evolved toward the possibility that matter was radically active."[18] Coming on the heels of baroque absolutism, the architecture of this period not only initiated the aesthetic and ideological transformations leading to neoclassicism but also rested on innovative approaches to the physical world.

These approaches presented some contrasting aspects. Matter seemed to be drawing in closer to humankind, since it functioned to turn the individual into a subject with self-awareness. Enlightenment materialists like Julien Offray de La Mettrie, Paul-Henri Thiry d'Holbach, and Denis Diderot went even further by rejecting the opposition between matter and mind. Yet this rapprochement paradoxically went hand in hand with the recognition of an irremediable otherness, which is why Condillac's sensationalist philosophy placed emphasis on the resistance of things to the sense of touch; seeing a table does not confirm its otherness from the self, but touching it does.

The understanding of materials reflected this ambivalence. On the one hand, matter seemed on the verge not only of revealing but, more than this, rendering possible previously inaccessible natural mechanisms and procedures. The understanding of strength of materials progressed with experiments like those conducted by the Dutch scientist Pieter van Musschenbroek and the French engineer Pierre-Simon Girard.[19] Chemistry made spectacular progress with Antoine Lavoisier and his study of oxidation. Metallurgy improved drastically also with the substitution of coke for charcoal in the smelting of iron ore, a practice that first emerged in 1709 in Coalbrookdale, England.[20] On the other hand, some important features of matter and materials remained unfathomable. Despite its vital importance for civil engineering and construction, the Enlightenment proved unable, for example, to penetrate the mystery surrounding the mechanism by which mortar hardened; this irritating enigma was not solved until the 1820s by scientists, engineers, and entrepreneurs such as Joseph Aspdin and Louis Vicat.[21] A property of matter that seemed to point toward some of its most fundamental aspects, possibly shared by living creatures, electricity remained even more mysterious, notwithstanding Benjamin Franklin's key insights. The Enlightenment saw the beginning of the belief in the relation between electricity and life, which found its full development at the time when Mary Shelley was writing her novel *Frankenstein*.

Overall, the Enlightenment was marked by technological optimism. On the threshold that separated the known and the unknown, practitioners, just like amateurs, grew more daring, embarking on material combinations that were unproven and often risky (such as the increasing use of reinforced stone in monumental structures). At its very beginning, iron construction was just as risky, involving untested assemblages of a material with properties that were far from stabilized.[22] Meanwhile, ingenious artisans experimented with all manner of artificial plaster and cardboard-based products.[23] In short, the technological optimism of the eighteenth century extended to newly malleable materials; people fashioned them as they pleased, casting aside age-old constraints in the name of an intimate relationship with matter. Simultaneously, the remaining opacity of matter and materials was often interpreted as a potential for unbounded progress, as if new properties and possibilities were just waiting for the inventor adventurous enough to discover them.

Architectural output in this period allows us to explore this duality of intimacy and otherness. Consider the regenerated architecture advocated by Boullée and Ledoux, which relied on the complicity they thought existed between the elementary forms that matter takes and the primary sensations that people feel. The endorsement of such a complicity came at a cost; other relationships were loosened, leading, for instance, to the unraveling of a long-standing reliance, established

A machine for testing the resistance of stone used by engineers and architects Émiland-Marie Gauthey, Jean-Rodolphe Perronet, and Jacques-Germain Soufflot during the construction of the Church of Sainte-Geneviève, now the Parisian Panthéon, in the 1770s, from Jean-Baptiste Rondelet, *Traité théorique et pratique de l'art de bâtir (Theoretical and Practical Treatise on the Art of Building)*, 1817. Investigation of the properties of materials ranked highly on the Enlightenment agenda.

in the fifteenth century, on proportions to govern not only buildings but also the human body and perception. One of the sure signs of this crisis was the undermining of the traditional notion of solidity based on the use of proportions sanctioned by Vitruvian theory and implemented in practice. Accompanied by the rediscovery of the lightness of Gothic construction, this undermining became evident with the polemics that arose regarding new bridges, such as those designed by the French engineer Jean-Rodolphe Perronet, as well as major monuments, like Jacques-Germain Soufflot's Church of Sainte-Geneviève. These constructions disregarded established rules about proportions, such as those between the span of arches and the width of the corresponding piers, and between the diameter of a cupola and the thickness of the pillars supporting it.[24] As we have seen, this change would enable the emergence of the notion of structure alongside its gradual dissociation from ornament.

The Enlightenment crisis of solidity also paved the way for the development of iron architecture, the slenderness of which far exceeded that of eighteenth-century stone bridges and churches, with their Gothic reference. The diffusion of cast iron, a material approximately sixty times more resistant to compression than the stone used by Perronet and Soufflot, marked the true end of the Vitruvian tradition. In the last decades of the eighteenth century, the use of iron was still highly experimental, situated beyond the traditional domain of architecture. The first English iron bridges, like Coalbrookdale's 1779 Iron Bridge and the 1796 Wearmouth Bridge, also known as the Sunderland Bridge, were more objects of curiosity than representative of common solutions to engineering problems.[25] Also located in England, the world's most technologically advanced country at the time, the first iron-framed buildings, including the 1797 Ditherington Mill in Shrewsbury and the North Mill in Belper, were developed in the same exploratory vein.[26]

The deliberate distancing from proportion in the Vitruvian sense spawned a novel set of analogies between matter and mind. Both now seemed imbricated in a series of calculated operations. As the French chemist Antoine Lavoisier's methodology revealed, material combinations could be compared with mathematical sums. Likewise, the procedural aggregation of elementary sensations generating complex ideas, as described by the English philosopher John Locke and his French follower Condillac, was deemed akin to some sort of mechanism of calculation, as though the mind operated like a machine for basic mathematical functions.[27] This is the context in which to situate the man-machine metaphor, which infused the writings of the physician and philosopher Julien Offray de La Mettrie, author of the treatise *L'Homme machine (Machine Man)* (1747), and the Marquis de Sade's various portraits of mechanistic copulation. This is likewise the context that causes some historians to cast the Enlightenment as an essential phase in the slow transformation of concepts of humanity that made cybernetics, and the very theme of the cyborg, possible.[28] It is no coincidence that Condillac's and Diderot's interest in touch and its relation with intellectual operations—an interest present, for instance, in Diderot's philosophical dialogues *Le Rêve de D'Alembert (D'Alembert's Dream)* (1769)—foreshadows the contemporary accent put on tactility. Touch appears indeed to be a major source of information on the outside world for the brain interpreted as a calculator.

Along with their calculatory character, combinations of matter and operations of the mind shared the common trait of generating movement and flow. This simultaneously calculatory and circulatory aspect has already been discussed in relation to the emergence of the notion of structure, which was linked to the rediscovery of Gothic architecture's specificities. In addition to lightness, or rather as its enabler, Gothic was characterized by the channeling of part of the thrust exerted by the vaults toward peripheral flying buttresses, a channeling that evoked the way water can be diverted in irrigation. In addition to vertical load paths, Gothic construction mobilized oblique stress lines that evoked immobile flows following complex patterns calling for precise calculation.[29]

In truth, the emphasis placed on circulation was much more widespread. As the physiologist and Freemason Pierre-Jean-Georges Cabanis asserted in his *Rapports du physique et du moral de l'homme (On the Relationship between the Physical and Moral Aspects of Man)* (1802): "Everything in nature is in constant motion; all bodies are in continuous flux.

Their elements combine and decompose; they successively take on a thousand fleeting forms: and these metamorphoses, which are the necessary outcomes of unceasing action, in turn renew the causes of this action and preserve the eternal youth of the universe."[30] The human mind—the inner workings of which Cabanis, like Locke and Condillac before him, aimed to discover—appeared to be just as fluid, motivated by combinations coming together and coming apart with the same ease as those of nature. Answering back to the "eternal youth of the universe" is the overall stability of the mind, without which self-awareness is not possible. Like the overall balance of nature, this stability is founded on myriad localized imbalances, ceaselessly unfolding compositions and decompositions. Between the laws of the physical world and those that govern the inner workings of the human mind, the structure of society itself seems to follow entirely comparable principles, if we are to believe the physiocrats and other pioneers of the discipline of economics; they describe a world of flows and exchanges that is at once stable and unstable, depending on the scale at which it is observed. This analogy between the dynamic workings of nature, those of society envisaged as the siege of endless circulation, and the similarly fluid operations of the mind replaced the old interpretation of the relation between macrocosm and microcosm. The introduction of society as a mediating turn between nature and humans was not only a change in conceptual frame. It also corresponded to the developments of various new practices, from economic policies to accounting techniques.[31]

The transformations marking the discipline of architecture circa 1800 fall within these broad parameters. By the time we get to Boullée's disciple, the architectural pedagogue Jean-Nicolas-Louis Durand, the emergence of composition as a design principle likewise functioned in response to the simultaneously calculatory and circulatory lens cast on mind and world.[32] Composition shares the same analytical orientation as sensualist philosophy initially gave the term; for Condillac, "analysis is . . . the entire decomposition of an object and the distribution of its parts in such a way that generation becomes easy."[33] In this scheme of things, to analyze is to attempt to decipher the fluctuating combinations of nature and humanity. For architecture, the emergence of the key notion of program is moored to the mechanisms of calculation and circulation haunting Enlightenment thought. For late eighteenth-century architects as well as for their successors, program was linked to the quantified assessment of need as well as to the consideration of the circulations generated by the different functional elements revealed by the analysis of the overall destination of the building.

Circulation and calculation characterized above all the structural approach that architecture shared with other disciplines like engineering. There is nothing surprising in the fact that nascent structural thinking in architecture sought to be analytical in the same way as chemistry, empiricist philosophy, and political economics. Indeed, where structure is concerned, this analytical character was reflected in the demand for the architectural legibility of load paths and transfers; hence the conviction that for each material—stone, wood, or iron—there is a corresponding structural type that best utilizes its mechanical properties. The assertion of "structural truth" or "truth to materials," initially posited by the Venetian Franciscan architectural theorist Carlo Lodoli (and later developed by Eugène-Emmanuel Viollet-le-Duc), stemmed from this conviction.[34]

This notion of structural truth or truth to materials is revealing of the progressive establishment of a new regime of materiality based on the contradictory intuitions that matter is both closer and more inscrutable to humans than what has been posited and experienced before. On the one hand, through materials and their use, going a step further than the common computability of nature and the human mind assumed by Enlightenment philosophy, matter seemed to partake in the human moral sphere, a conception admirably conveyed by John Ruskin in the chapter devoted to the "Lamp of Truth" in his *Seven Lamps of Architecture*. On the other hand, matter appeared at times not only opaque but also animated by nonhuman forces to be reckoned with, forces synonymous with a truth that could actually have nothing to do with ordinary morality. In other words, did structural truth constitute an ethical value, or was it more akin to a natural principle, or perhaps both? The question was never clearly answered.

In our contemporary moment, architects and engineers are increasingly relinquishing the idea that there is a truth to materials that preexists their use, and this offers one of the clearest signs that the terms of another regime of materiality are being configured in our very midst. This calling into question of constructional truth is shaking the concept of tectonics to its very core, precisely because designers now entertain the possibility of endowing matter with properties that were previously considered mutually exclusive, such as transparency and structural resistance or insulating capacity—a possibility that has given birth to composite materials.

This current change in attitudes is embedded in the longer historical process of modernity's arrival. The close links among architecture, construction, and engineering that Enlightenment analytical methods postulated began to loosen in the first decades of the nineteenth century, which saw the disciplines of physics and mathematics definitively distance themselves from the geometrical know-how to which architecture remained faithful.[35] Although both architects and engineers recognized the pertinence of the notion of structure, the gap widened between (following Condillac) "the entire decomposition of an object and the distribution of its parts in such a way that generation becomes easy"—in other words, the analytical mode of decomposition, recomposition, and distribution that remained at the heart of the architectural project—and mathematical analysis based on calculus. It was on calculus that emerging engineering disciplines such as rational mechanics and strength of materials were based, and this led to a radical rethinking of what constitutes *firmitas,* or the solidity of buildings. Yet underlying the conflict-inducing tensions between engineers (who relied on the mathematical analysis of integrals with complex limits) and architects (who remained attached to the animation of matter through geometry) was a permanent shift in the regime of analogies between matter and humanity upon which architects had erected the givens of design ever since the Renaissance.

This new regime was permeated with tensions and contradictions. On this ground also, structural truth proved revealing. Ruskin epitomized its fundamental ambiguity when he chose to exclude iron from the list of materials noble enough to deserve architectural treatment. Was structural truth a subjective notion without genuine material basis? To complicate the question further, architects were often obliged to take liberties with structural truth, understood in a literal way, in order to express fully the higher-level intuition that guided their use of a given material. The American architect Louis Sullivan provided a striking example of this type of trade-off with his 1891 Wainwright Building in St. Louis, which Frank Lloyd Wright considered to be the "very first human expression of a tall steel office-building as Architecture," where one slender brick pier of the façades out of two does not correspond to a steel column.[36] However, the rapid rhythm of these piers conveys more convincingly the nervous spirit of the steel frame than what a looser spacing would have achieved.[37] When trying to address issues of materiality, architecture is often led to such compromises. More generally, the relation between architecture and construction depends on the narratives used by designers to enroll technology, from materials to structure, in their projects. Sullivan's conception of the tall office building is partly a narrative, or, to put it in more radical terms, a fiction. Instead of truth, one often faces such narratives or fictions.[38]

It is worth concluding this brief series of historical sketches, which is crucially motivated by architecture's relation to materiality, with a few words on the advent of the twentieth century. In my earlier discussion of the animation of matter, I sought to underscore the connections to be made between modernist architecture and the rise of a mechanized society in which the automobile played a highly symbolic role (even though it was but one in a vast number of industrialized objects and technical processes that profoundly altered the human relationship to the world). In *Mechanization Takes Command* (1948), Sigfried Giedion fulfilled his role as an official voice for modernism by insisting on the all-encompassing character of a phenomenon that concerned everything from agriculture and domestic chores to industry and modes of transport.[39] The rise of modern architecture dovetailed with a change in materiality, which made possible yet another approach to materials. From concrete to steel, materials now functioned to allow architecture as a discipline to keep in step with a movement that was

Louis Sullivan, Wainwright Building, St. Louis, Missouri, 1891. The "very first human expression of a tall steel office-building as Architecture," as Frank Lloyd Wright had it, was also a construction transgressing the code of structural truth. HABS MO.96-SAL.49-4, Library of Congress.

sweeping across the globe, all the while avoiding being dissolved by it. Concrete, in particular, was invested with this double mission; it had the capacity to take on innovative and daring forms yet still remain "artificial stone," a successor to masonry (unless its use is seen to be derived from the even more ancient employment of compacted and molded earth, or adobe, which some of its properties undeniably bring to mind).[40] This was the explanation Giedion offered in one of his early books, *Bauen in Frankreich, Bauen in Eisen, Bauen in Eisenbeton (Building in France, Building in Iron, Building in Ferroconcrete)* (1928), in which he both emphasized the innovative character of the structures designed in the new material (by Auguste Perret, Anatole de Baudot, Tony Garnier, and Le Corbusier) and repositioned them within a national tradition of research into structural performance that, to his mind, dated back to Gothic achievements.[41]

Epitomized by the use of concrete and steel, the attitude of modernist architects toward matter oscillated between two opposite poles. On the one hand, new technological possibilities allowed matter to appear as a resource that could be mobilized at will. With the development of thin shells in the 1930s by pioneers like Eduardo Torroja and Robert Maillart, for instance, concrete seemed pliable in ways that would have been difficult to foresee decades earlier.[42] On the other hand, "truth to materials" implied the existence of principles or even rules that bounded the imagination of designers. The tension was never actually solved between a Promethean relation to the material world and greater attention paid to its inner principles.

The proponents of modernist architecture realized early on that the evolution in which they participated would not leave human beings' relation to the world unaltered. Even so, some needs seemed to endure or even grow more robust in the context of a mechanized society that was increasingly urbanized. In the ever-expanding city, air, light, and contact with nature proved more vital than ever. Questions thus needed to be posed about what had endured and what needed to be changed. Change itself could lead to a whole new world order or, on the contrary, engender a restoration of living conditions that had been momentarily curbed by industrial advancements.

By the same token, the subject being addressed by modernist architecture was placed in a state of tension—or, more precisely, of contradiction—that was difficult to overcome. From one point of view, the modern human condition seemed profoundly different from, and even superior to, what had preceded it; it is no accident that the Nietzschean figure of the *Übermensch,* or superman, haunted the thoughts of the young Charles-Édouard Jeanneret, soon to be known by the pseudonym Le Corbusier.[43] In addition, the influence of biological and social Darwinism in the first decades of the twentieth century makes clear how prominent modernist architects came to be receptive to eugenics, which was being popularized and institutionalized by such figures as the American biologist Charles Davenport and the French surgeon and biologist Alexis Carrel.[44] This racially based vantage, which fueled a broader perception of human beings as unhealthy and even sick, explains the deliberately hygiene-oriented character of modernist architecture as well as the popularity enjoyed by the program of sanatoriums, which sought to serve as machines for healing through exposure to light and air (this agenda was foremost, for example, in the Finnish architect and designer Alvar Aalto's Paimio Sanatorium, completed in 1932). The fascination with transparency followed this same logic, driving designers such as Ludwig Mies van der Rohe to take an interest in X-rays, the symbol of a nearly absolute transparency invested with curative properties.[45]

From an architectural standpoint, there was something utterly contradictory about designing buildings that were intended to serve a superior humanity as well as an ailing one, as if both had the same needs: Was it possible to address potential supermen and tuberculosis sufferers simultaneously? This polarization was only intensified when questions emerged concerning the overall ambition of the modernist enterprise: Was the aim to revolutionize the order of things so as to hasten the advent of a "better" humanity? Or, against this delusion of grandeur, was it a matter of regenerating industrial society by reviving certain essential values that had been waylaid over the course of its onward march? Revolution or restoration? Avant-garde or conservation? The ambiguity of modernist architecture arguably lies in its failure to

Alvar Aalto, solarium at Paimio Sanatorium, 1928–32. Photograph by Gustaf Welin, Alvar Aalto Museum, 1930s. Aalto's sanatorium is emblematic of modernism's dual view of the human body: its heroic interpretation finds its counterpart in an obsession with the ailing human being.

offer conclusive answers to these questions—hence the uncertainty with regard to nature, the incongruity of a will to sever and renew all at once the ties to the natural world. This was made manifest in the modern buildings and cities that rose up heroically, all the while enacting a harmonious contract between natural and built realms. This was the case with Ebenezer Howard's garden city movement, and the relationship between the latter and modern urbanism was discernible in the Broadacre City proposals elaborated by Frank Lloyd Wright beginning in the 1930s as well as in many other projects, built and unbuilt.[46] In the final analysis, if modern buildings and cities fell under the aegis of a quest for purification, as Bruno Latour among others has proposed, they likewise reflected an entirely opposite impulse consisting in seeking out a hybrid condition in which the human partially works its way back to the nonhuman.

These contradictions were not all specific to architecture. Some of them reflected the profound ambivalence of the subject in the machine era—a subject who was simultaneously glorified and weakened by the appliances that populated and structured everyday life. To return to the automobile, this was a machine that produced sensations of power—think of the exhilarating impression produced by acceleration—and feelings of vulnerability, because a car accident, with all kinds of dire physical consequences, was always possible. Similarly, the impact of the two world wars should not be overlooked, given the shocking stream of dead, injured, and mutilated individuals they left behind. In the aftermath of 1918, the haunting presence of the maimed—the "broken faces"—in the towns and villages of Germany and France was a traumatic reminder of the fragilities of machine-era civilization and of the subjectivity to which it gave rise.

Another contradiction marking the formation of the subject in the machine era stemmed from the collision of, on the one hand, the rise of highly individualized aspirations (some of which were expressed through car driving or achievement in sport) and, on the other, the increasingly significant role of the social category of the undifferentiated masses (to which the related rise of totalitarian regimes and modern media in the first half of the twentieth century attested). From the authorship of individual destiny to the particle lost in a crowd overdetermined by political and economic systems—modern architecture tested out all sorts of compromises in an attempt to reconcile these extremes.

The point is that in the modern age, architecture and urbanism sought out the glories of an epic stature while also betraying a deep awareness of the tragic fragilities of the heroic model on which they were based. Modernism is haunted through and through by the question of correct proportions and the unit of measure that lies at the heart of a world that had seemingly lost its bearings—in no small part because of such things as the "twentyfold speeds" of the automobile to which Le Corbusier continually referred, as well as the standardization of a whole range of dimensions of social life. This nagging issue of measure and commensurability explains the celebratory reception of the German art historian Rudolf Wittkower's *Architectural Principles in the Age of Humanism* (1949) by a modern movement nevertheless averse to historicism. By studying the role of proportion in Andrea Palladio's architecture, Wittkower reinforced the modernist quest for a unit of measure adequate to the task of rigorously assessing a brave new postwar world; it was in this same moment, after all, that Le Corbusier conceived of his Modulor system.[47] If there is irony in this context, then, it lies in the fact that modern architecture and urbanism were often criticized for their excessiveness. This cannot be attributed solely to the rerouting of ideals that were undoubtedly too ambitious to be held for long. In hindsight, it also appears to be an inevitable consequence of the cumulative contradictions affecting the individual to whom architectural and urban modernism were addressed.

Now, if the key historical moments briefly surveyed here serve to highlight what one can usefully view as changing regimes of materiality, they likewise bear witness to a substantial shift in the relationship between architecture and language. At each of these historical junctures, the status accorded to ornament, which is one of the primary means at architecture's disposal to animate matter, reflected the problem of adequately communicating architecture's ambitions.

To begin with, remember that the question of language was already present in the work of Vitruvius. His treatise found its source in a Hellenistic culture that was convinced of the preeminence of discursive reason, or *logos,* over and above other forms of thought and action—a culture that, by the same token, considered philosophy, eloquence, and poetry to be superior to other forms of cultural or artistic expression (such as, of course, architecture, the most material of the arts). As a result, *De architectura* betrays a desire to bind architecture to discursive reasoning; Vitruvius clearly favored proportions based on rational numbers that could be expressed through ordinary language rather than those that called on irrational numbers such as pi or the square root of two, which are obtained through geometric constructions—that is, through manual exercises like drawing a circle or a diagonal.[48]

Renaissance architectural theorists, too, were driven by an ambition to orchestrate convincingly a rapprochement between architecture and a humanist culture centered on the spoken and written word. However, they arguably devised a more sophisticated set of methods than those developed by Vitruvius. It should be stressed that unlike the latter, prominent figures such as Alberti and Daniele Barbaro were more properly humanists than builders. According to them, architecture ultimately originated in *logos*—and in this regard, it is important to stress that in Alberti's writings, as in those of Filarete, this discursive raison d'être took on a dialogical character; in both theory and practice, architecture appears as the outcome of a set of conversations between past and present authors as well as between cultured architects and their powerful patrons.[49] Manifold bridges were built between architecture and language in this period: some were based on the ancient tradition of the art of memory (which consists in using sequences of places, like rooms in a building, to memorize endless lists of elements); others, on the relationship between rhetoric and architecture (which allowed Philibert de l'Orme to place the figure of the modern architect—a notion he sought to promote—under the protection of the god Mercury, "creator of eloquence").[50] Yet the closest ties were formed by means of the written word in the penning and printing of treatises. As the architectural historian Mario Carpo has demonstrated, architecture as a discipline is both the heir to antiquity and the offspring of printing, which, from the Renaissance onward, enabled the wide diffusion of principles and patterns.[51]

Ornamentation in the Vitruvian tradition—from the Hellenistic period to the end of the seventeenth century—thus bears the imprint of a complex network placing architecture and language in relation to each other. Ornament oscillates between its status as an element caught up in a system of differentiations (which calls to mind linguistic articulations) and its function as an autonomous signifier (or symbol in its own right). That is to say, ornament must be subjected to rules just as it needs to assert freedom from them. When robbed of the capacity to deviate from the rules—when left to operate without "license," to use Sebastiano Serlio's term—no art can stand firm.[52]

Above all, ornament is effective only when it blurs the boundary between making and expression. Put another way, it is neither structural nor decorative, embodying instead the order and measure that serve as the basis for architecture's meaningfulness.

Some final reflections on the "speaking architecture" of the second half of the eighteenth century are needed here. The desire to speak caused the architecture of the Enlightenment to take paths that were different from those explored in the Renaissance: on the one hand, it was informed by an ambition to go back to the origin of language—and even to what preceded that origin—in order to access the primary sensations that nature impresses on the human mind; on the other hand, it was motivated by a forward movement toward a symbolism sustained by mythology and history. This dual tendency enabled the gradual dissociation of structure and ornament, which left its trace on the discipline of architecture from that moment forth. Structural concerns and architectural decoration rarely mingled in practice, yet Vitruvian-inspired ornament, beginning with the five orders, had until then guaranteed the existence of unifying principles for the process of animating matter. Yet if nineteenth-century architects continued to use the orders intensively, they never managed to restore a definitively jeopardized unity.

It is in this context that the impact of the modernist architect's rejection of ornament must be assessed. The rejection caused the discipline finally to become coherent again at the same time it authorized the members of a new generation to challenge in unison the outrageous ornamentalism of the nineteenth century (which seemed to them comparable to some sort of prattling that concealed architecture's true message). Modernist architecture, in short, sought out expression by means other than those that had previously served as the wellspring of the animation of matter. Once ornament had been relinquished, what remained in the architect's grasp was structure, otherwise known as tectonics. In order to mark a difference from the authority of the engineer, which had been on the rise since the second half of the eighteenth century, architecture gradually reorganized tectonics around the notion of space.[53] The collusion between architecture and language, for which traditional ornamentation had served as vehicle, was replaced by a desire for expression based on a form of logic that was more scientific than linguistic in nature, as well as on emotions that appeared prior to speech. Modernist designers were guided as much by physical laws and social statistics as by the experiential apprehension of the fundamental principles of the discipline (such as matter, structure, light, and space). Like the matter and structure that the designer transformed with the assistance of light, space was meant to be "ineffable," as Le Corbusier famously put it.[54]

Is such a position tenable in the long term? Is it really possible to renounce ornament and thereby find liberation from linguistic temptation? It is interesting to note that the ornamental dimension remains ever present in the work of Adolf Loos and Mies in their use of precious materials such as marble and onyx. Not coincidentally, Mies's structural detail often seems to take up the linguistic articulations of the classical orders. Many other aspects of modernist production are likewise ornamental in character, including color and, above all, furniture design, as Alina Payne has shown in her study of ornament circa 1900.[55] By the same token, modernist architects were constantly speaking at conferences, conventions, and artistic gatherings. They published manifestos, articles, and books with sustained regularity, and in so doing, they moved outside the domain of scientific reasoning, beyond the realm of emotions preceding language. When some went so far as to venture into poetry, it was not always easy to discern the dividing line between their words and the forms they conjured up. The question of language thus continued to haunt designers, even though they had demonstrated a desire to overcome its limiting effects. Is it any wonder that Bruno Zevi so insistently called for modern architecture to be built into a language?[56] The quest for the ineffable and the desire to speak proved to be intimately tied.

Throughout the history that has been roughly sketched out here, it is possible to pick out similarities lurking beyond the major rifts that have punctuated its unfolding. For instance, the modernist commitment to both the ineffable and the scientific echoes the Enlightenment

Ludwig Mies van der Rohe, Barcelona Pavilion, 1929 (reconstruction, 1986). There is something distinctively ornamental in the use of precious materials such as marble, red onyx, and travertine in this emblematic realization of modernist architecture.

desire for a mode of architectural expression that is both upstream and downstream from language. I will later argue that the rejection of symbolism that characterizes our current era actually takes up the modernist utopian premise of architecture's capacity to express itself without any reference whatsoever to language—with the caveat that a certain form of monumental ornament characterizes whole swaths of contemporary production.

These similarities and differences—these echoes, revivals, and irrevocable breaks that mark successive regimes of materiality—are worth examining in a more systematic way than has been outlined here. Above all, such studies should be carried beyond the Western tradition. Materiality in all its dimensions—in terms of the animation of matter, linguistic articulations, and ornamental negotiations, all of them inseparable from the consideration of the human subject whom architecture tries to address—is a vital part of any rigorous cross-cultural study of architectural questions. The concept of materiality has the potential to bolster the comparison of concerns, problems, and solutions according to an analytical framework that avoids juxtaposing Welsh towers, Chinese pagodas, and Hindu temples in the manner of an encyclopedia. By addressing broadly shared dimensions that move beyond questions of program and style, scholars might write another global history of architecture.

5

Architecture and Materiality in the Digital Era

The next step in this synoptic consideration of the relationships among architecture, matter, and language turns to the contemporary moment and the transformations that have taken place with the rise of digital media in design practices. As with the episodes in architecture's history touched upon in the preceding chapters, what needs to be addressed is how these transformations reflect a change in materiality, the umbrella concept under which our analysis falls. However one assesses the aesthetic and technological merits of so-called digital architecture and its globalization, most of its proponents have a fairly keen awareness of this umbrella concept. This is evidenced in the frequent references to the "new materialism" made by such authors as the Mexican American philosopher Manuel De Landa and the Canadian-born architectural theorist Sanford Kwinter; it is likewise seen in evocations of an architecture imbued with such natural properties as "complexity" and "emergence," which are very different in kind from the characteristics traditionally attributed to the natural world.[1]

Contemporary engagements with questions of animation, which have surfaced with renewed intensity—especially since the publication of such writings as *Animate Form* (1999), by the American architect and theorist Greg Lynn—fall into this same perspective.[2] For the matter that practitioners of digital architecture set out to address is fundamentally animated, capable of self-organization and collaboration with the designer. We will return to this collaborative ideal, for it is crucially supported by the computer. Indeed, the use of machines as design tools in their own right is a relatively recent phenomenon in the field of architecture, having appeared decisively in the 1990s. While a number of pioneering experiments had been carried out earlier, it was not until this period that architectural teaching and practice started to change significantly.[3] For example, the launch of the "paperless studio" in 1994 at Columbia University's Graduate School of Architecture, Planning, and Preservation is often taken as a defining moment in this shift. Computers took the place of drawing and tracing paper, and, as the French architect and former Columbia dean Bernard Tschumi recalled with a smile in a 2004 interview:

> That is a great name, but we generated a lot of paper! Well, we decided to introduce the computers in 1994–95 and we said that every student was going to have a computer. Before there were computer labs, but we were the first to bring computers into the studios. In other words, the idea was that all of the work would be done on computers and there would be no paper. But then the plotters were introduced . . .[4]

Despite the narrow time frame, the transformations wrought by the digitization of architectural design have proved to be profound. Given the scale and ubiquity of these changes, it is sometimes difficult to imagine that barely twenty-five years ago most design work was still carried out by hand. At the start of this evolution away from paper, formal aspects were the ones that demanded the most attention: in particular, the appearance of new geometries based on smooth curves controlled using splines, for which Lynn coined the term "blob."[5] Notably successful expressions of this formal mode are built projects such as the Water Pavilion designed by Lars Spuybroek's firm NOX, which opened in 1993 on Neeltje Jans, an artificial island in the province of Zeeland in the Netherlands; Peter Cook and Colin Fournier's Kunsthaus Graz (2003) in Austria; and the Selfridges Building (2003) in Birmingham, England, by Future Systems. Yet despite the innovative quality of such

NOX/Lars Spuybroek, HtwoOexpo, also known as the Water Pavilion, Neeltje Jans, the Netherlands, 1993–97, interior view. This structure is emblematic of the first generation of digital architecture, with curvilinear geometries and a "home for cyborgs" ambiance.

examples, the vast majority of projects designed by means of computer programs continued to look just like earlier buildings. The process that produced architecture, however, began to set itself apart definitively from traditional working methods and means of representation.

Speculation on the nature of the transformations under way subsequently crystallized around the flexibility of digital tools and their ability to shift from one-off solutions to families of forms through the variation of certain defining parameters. First envisioned by French poststructuralist theorists—in particular the philosopher Gilles Deleuze and the architect and industrial designer Bernard Cache—as the instrument of a break from modernist norms, digital architecture's capacity to instigate potentially infinite variation was the central theme of a 2003 Centre Pompidou exhibition curated by the philosopher and critic Frédéric Migayrou.[6] Variation underlies the notion of "parametricism" that Patrik Schumacher, collaborator and successor of the Iraqi British architect Zaha Hadid, has been trying to impose for a number of years. For Schumacher, the exploration of variation governed by well-chosen parameters signals the advent of an unprecedented style that enables the design techniques characteristic of the digital era to align with social, political, and economic aspirations—and at all scales (from pieces of furniture to skyscrapers).[7]

The past decade has been marked mainly by an increasing number of reflections on digital fabrication. The Swiss architectural firm founded by Matthias Kohler and Fabio Gramazio has received worldwide attention for its robot-assembled installations.[8] As the firm's website emphasizes:

> We do not design architecture solely by drawing, but conceive spatial relationships and contextual behaviour through programming. In doing so, we use the potentials of the computer and of digital fabrication

Robotic arm in operation, Gramazio Kohler Research, ETH Zurich, 2008. Copyright Gramazio Kohler Research, ETH Zurich. The development of digital fabrication marked a decisive shift from the geometric speculation of the early years of digital architecture to an active engagement with material issues.

> complementary to traditional design, construction and building methods. The sensual quality of this design culture manifests itself in the novel expression of a Digital Materiality.[9]

In a similar vein, designers such as Achim Menges and Jenny Sabin have explored the relationships between natural processes and algorithms, arguing that these are a manifestation of "material computation," a calculatory dimension that is ostensibly widespread in the physical world and that designers should therefore exploit. As we will see, this perspective, while recalling some of the ways in which Enlightenment thought made calculation a fundamental component of nature, reflects a profound change in attitude toward the physical world—one involving a collaboration with it rather than an aspiration to dominate it.

Recently, in close relation with digital fabrication and the perspectives opened by machine learning and artificial intelligence, a series of young designers, such as Gilles Retsin, have abandoned the smooth forms that characterized the first age of digital architecture in favor of a direct expression of the computer power of aggregation of discrete elements, possibly assembled by robots. To characterize this shift from continuous inflections to discontinuous, often brutal assemblages, Mario Carpo has introduced the terms "digital discrete" and "discretism."[10]

Blobs, parametricism, digital fabrication, "nonstandard" architecture, "discretism"—these denotations of the transformations marking the discipline, pervasive as they are becoming, would seem to present two major limitations. First, they are directed only at a small portion of contemporary architectural output—that which identifies itself as a digital avant-garde—without clarifying how all this relates to the majority of buildings designed by architects using computers. The assumption is that the connections are self-evident (when they are not), and pioneering proposals are bound to prevail simply on the basis of their presumed audacity and clear-sightedness. Yet the small if spectacular minority of buildings that are emblematic of this way of envisioning the discipline remains far removed from the vast majority of projects designed simply with the aid of computers; in this respect, "digital architecture" remains deeply ambiguous. In addition, the digital avant-garde fails to

Institute for Computational Design and Construction and Institute of Building Structures and Structural Design at the University of Stuttgart Research Pavilion, 2016–17, detail. Conceived and realized under the supervision of Achim Menges, one of the main proponents of the material computation movement, the pavilion makes innovative use of fiber composite materials.

Gilles Retsin Architecture, Karlsplatz I, project for a museum extension, Vienna, 2015, detail. Such architecture is emblematic of the shift toward discontinuous, often brutal assemblages, which the theorist and historian Mario Carpo interprets as a "second digital turn" related to the rise of machine learning.

acknowledge sufficiently the necessary connection between the evolution of the discipline and the far more widespread dynamic caused by the advent of digital culture. This is a dynamic that touches all aspects of existence, from everyday life to industrial manufacturing, from transportation to politics, and from popular culture to the emotional relationships we form with each other.

In order to assess what is occurring with greater accuracy, perhaps we need to reconsider the tools themselves, beginning with the computer, while avoiding the trap of technological determinism. As historians are well aware, the information society was not created by the computer; rather, it began to appear in the last decades of the nineteenth century with the spectacular surge of data necessary for the proper functioning of economic and political entities, of businesses and bureaucracies.[11] In other words, the information society is what rendered useful, even indispensable, the invention of a machine like the computer (after having given rise to, in turn, the typewriter, the tabulator, and other countless devices for recording, processing, and recovering data). Yet in order to avoid moving straight from technological to sociocultural determinism, it is surely best to speak of the "coproduction," as the scholar of science and technology studies Sheila Jasanoff has put it, of society on the one hand and information and communications technologies on the other.[12] The computer is the tip of the iceberg, just one component of a far greater dynamic.

The changing interpretations of the nature, purpose, and use value of the computer are good indications of the direction this dynamic has taken. In the early years of its existence, almost half a century before its use became widespread in architectural firms, the computer was envisaged as a machine whose primary function was calculation. It was invented specifically for that purpose during World War II, and its first applications in Great Britain and the United States moved in that direction (from deciphering Nazi codes to developing the hydrogen bomb).[13] However, it was not long before the computer seemed akin to an artificial brain capable of logical reasoning. It is worth remembering that as early as 1949, this analogy loomed large in the book *Giant Brains, or Machines That Think,* by Edmund Berkeley, cofounder of the Association for Computing Machinery.[14] Over the course of the following decade, the mathematician and philosopher Norbert Wiener's cybernetics cemented the place of the computer at the heart of an approach to the world that positioned humans and machines within a single conceptual paradigm based on bits of information and feedback loops.[15] It is also worth remembering, along these lines, that while the

English term *computer* signifies a capacity for calculation, the French term *ordinateur*—coined by a Sorbonne philologist in 1955 at the request of a former student who had become head of IBM France—refers instead to a capacity for logical sequencing.[16]

In the wake of calculation and logical sequencing, a third interpretation of the computer has emerged in more recent decades—just as the digital realm has extended far beyond its traditional applications in computing and hybridized with objects of everyday life such as the telephone, giving birth to the smartphone, as well as spreading to cars, elevators, televisions, and washing machines. At the core of this ever more extensive presence, computers and, more broadly, the digital realm appear as a form of technology that is overhauling our relationship with physical reality in a comprehensive way, starting with the sensory sphere: the way we, early twenty-first-century humans, see, hear, smell, taste, and touch the things around us. To begin with, we can no longer see without being decisively influenced by digital cameras; whether stand-alone instruments or integrated into our telephones, they are substitutes for our eyes, and we are now habituated to images that seem to be perfectly focused regardless of distance. We listen to compressed digital audio files, we send messages on Snapchat that disappear almost instantaneously, and we wear fragrances that have been synthesized with the aid of sophisticated software that enables perfume makers to combine scents in the same way that designers use graphics programs to juggle forms and colors. Indeed, the list of ways in which the human relationship to the physical world has been transformed by the digital is simply astonishing. Zooming in and out now seems almost as natural as blinking. The scale of phenomena often becomes problematic in the sense that we can shift almost instantaneously from the infinitely small to the infinitely large.

Interestingly, the American architects Charles and Ray Eames, who were trailblazers in their thinking about the relationship between computers and architecture, caught a glimpse of this latter evolution in their 1977 documentary *Powers of Ten,* which offers a vertiginous voyage from galaxies to atoms. Yet Google Earth has since made this seem banal. The boundary between the abstraction of numbers and pure sensation is becoming increasingly blurred (music in digital formats testifies to this). We are entering a world of sensory givens, which is marked by the effects of synesthesia. Forms appear to become tactile, and sounds gustatory. Neuroscience is exploring the biological and cognitive foundations of this multisensory world in which for example, the blind can be made to "see" in different ways (through engagement of the sensitivity of the skin or the tongue, for instance).

It is no accident that I have slipped imperceptibly from a grasp of the material world into an understanding of humans supported by recent studies in neuroscience. Indeed, digital technologies reflect the *joint* transformation of the perception of the physical world and the interpretation of what constitutes the human. Like the automobile before them, these technologies are contributing to the ways in which we understand materiality. They are closely linked to a definition of phenomena and objects that now includes emergence mechanisms, digital files, genetic codes, and the software platforms of Web 2.0. Above all, we are witnessing the unstoppable evolution of an approach that sees materiality as inevitably bound to happenings, situations, and events rather than to stable substances. The information bit is never more than an elementary occurrence, or an "atom of circumstance," as the French philosopher Pierre Lévy put it.[17] Data are organized around happenings that aggregate into situations and bring about events, and, as I will argue, this mode of understanding the world is having a profound impact on architecture.

The very contact with these different types of aggregate and data-driven "things" means that humans reveal themselves to be different. Information and communications technologies go hand in hand with a representation of contemporary women and men as intimately associated with technology. Since the 1950s, the figure of the cyborg has embodied this situation of intimacy, which can go as far as hybridization.[18] Initially developed in laboratories, the cyborg was taken up in popular culture with resounding success; Hollywood films such as *The Terminator* (1984) and *RoboCop* (1987) are fictional accounts of the blending of flesh and machine, of course, but remember that the Vitruvian man portrayed in the Renaissance was already the product of a process of idealization. Today, such fictions present us with the image of futurity, with what we are set to become, and with something akin to the transhumanist dreams of Raymond Kurzweil, the American theorist of the "singularity," bearing witness to rampant technological progress as humans finally attain the ability to upload their personalities to servers and thus achieve immortality.[19] The plans for the biomedical supervision of individuals currently being contemplated by corporate giants of the digital, such as Apple and Google, fall within the same parameters (and it is no surprise that Kurzweil is an adviser to Google's management team).

Over the past few years, the cyborg appears to have been replaced by a networked personality that resides simultaneously within and outside the body; distributed through neural networks that ensure the proper functioning of the mind, it is at the same time spread across numerous physical and electronic channels that connect it to the environment. This vision of the networked individual has been explored by, among others, the performance artist Stelarc, who extends his body in multiple ways through mechanical exoskeletons and electronic devices. This kind of foray into the extension and potential obsolescence of the physical body is quite similar to later insights about cybernetics, such as those described by the anthropologist and systems theorist Gregory Bateson in *Steps to an Ecology of Mind* (1972); Bateson suggests that the contemporary individual should be understood as an ecology, a sort of viewpoint or perspective on the world, rather than as an entity with inexorably defined boundaries.[20] In this sense, Condillac's statue appears to have been replaced by a subjectivity that spreads through numerous channels instead of waiting for the arrival of external stimuli, as does the spider poised in the middle of its web. The latter metaphor for intelligence is contemporaneous with Condillac's aforementioned *Treatise on the Sensations* and was evoked, for example, in Denis Diderot's *Le Rêve de D'Alembert.*

The transition from the man-machine, or cyborg, to the individual who is connected in multiple ways to an environment (as opposed to separate from it) goes hand in hand with a shift in attitude toward the physical world. This shift is important specifically because it allows for a more detailed elaboration of a regime of materiality that is emerging before our very eyes. This regime is inseparable from ethical prescriptions and should therefore lead to different behaviors and a genuine reform of the ways in which we design and take action. For what is closely linked to our increasing sensitivity toward environmental issues is a calling into question of the modernist vision of the heroism of human will that beats the physical world into submission. What emerges to replace this antagonistic fiction is an ideal of collaboration with the forces animating matter, or, more precisely, with the forces that course through and animate the human and nonhuman alike, newly considered as continuous entities. Philosophy and sociology have contributed to elucidating the theoretical presuppositions of this attitude: for example, the fundamentally continuous vision of the world offered by Deleuze and Félix Guattari, and accounts of the nonhuman actors with which humans constantly have to cope offered by actor network theory proponents Michel Callon and Bruno Latour.[21] Surely, the claim goes, nonhuman objects and phenomena should be considered independent actors rather than mere resources to be drawn on at will. This nascent ideal of collaboration evidently relates to the "new materialism" and the "material turn" that have left a profound imprint on contemporary humanities and social sciences. It has led to attempts by the anthropologist Tim Ingold and the sociologist Richard Sennett, among others, to revive the figure of the artisan who works in harmony with matter as opposed to imposing arbitrary plans on it. As Ingold explains, the creative process ought to be visualized "longitudinally, as a confluence of forces and materials, rather than laterally, as a transposition from images to object."[22]

In architecture, such a stance is probably more ideological than practical, or rather more akin to an ideal than to an everyday reality, insofar as matter and materials remain always resistant and opaque as soon as one leaves the domain of speculation and experiment to engage the complexity of concrete construction processes. Nevertheless, this kind of thinking exerts a strong seduction today. Many designers active in the digital avant-garde have embraced it. It is present, for example, in the Dutch architect and artist Lars Spuybroek's *The Sympathy of Things: Ruskin and the Ecology of Design* (2011); the "sympathy" Spuybroek sets out to promote rests precisely on the collaborative ideal just described.[23] Likewise, the concept of material computation developed from entirely similar concerns, and a more general trend (following Ingold et al.) bears witness to the ways in which digital makers strongly identify with the figure of the artisan as well as with a credo of collaboration with physical objects and phenomena. A new design ethic is coming to the fore, albeit one riven with contradiction in the sense that digital fabrication can also be interpreted as the ultimate manifestation of a demiurgic desire to impose one's views on matter by injecting it with information from files developed well prior to its fashioning. However, if the most fervent followers of digital fabrication are to be believed, such a desire plays a secondary role in the development of what they readily present as the emergence of a novel relationship to the world—a relationship that fab labs (fabrication laboratories) set out to promote.[24] The question of architectural expression thus needs to be posed differently: Instead of seeking to animate matter in a perfectly artificial way, how might designers facilitate its spontaneous expressive capacity and thereby channel this potential in such a way as to align it with formal intentions?

The frequent evocation of emergence by the digital avant-garde refers precisely to this capacity for spontaneous animation—to the possibility of patterns issuing forth, often suddenly, within a system that initially appears to be without order or structure.[25] Animation in the digital era sets out to be more fundamental or intrinsic to matter than the approach that relies on the identification of parts, members, or organs. What is more, a whole array of contemporary digital designs is tending to substitute the definition of parametric relationships for the identification of parts, members, or organs.[26] As the architectural historian Spyros Papapetros convincingly observes in his study of animation in the arts and architecture circa 1900, the desire on the part of the digital avant-garde to mobilize the self-organizing capacities of matter sometimes seems to reengage with the various earlier attempts at "animation of the inorganic" that are the focus of his book.[27]

The evolution of materiality is inseparable from a more general change in our concept of nature, which has so shaken long-held convictions that it deserves highlighting. What we mean by nature today calls into question a set of associations that have hitherto formed our basic representations of the world—for instance, the assumption that calculability is synonymous with predictability. This equivalence is spectacularly challenged by the dynamic systems we are now discovering at all scales (from those governing microcellular mechanisms to those influencing the evolution of the cosmos). Conversely, ancient antinomies, such as the opposition between the organic and the mechanical, are losing their efficacy; some vital processes, derived as they are from complex algorithms, bear a strong resemblance to mechanisms. The boundary between these traditionally distinct orders of reality is being blurred at countless junctures, generating unsettling ambiguities; take, for example, genetically modified organisms, which can be considered living beings just as easily as they can be seen as human-made products. Even if we are no longer as invested as we once were in direct analogies between the brain and the computer (in spite of the latter's simulation of human reasoning), there no longer seems to be any ontological opposition between biological processes and mechanical functions.

While some oppositions are dying away, others are taking on unprecedented prominence. Our contemporary concept of nature is thus marked by a permanent tension between a fundamentally continuous vision of phenomena and that which allows us to give an account of these phenomena—that is, discrete tools that are necessarily discontinuous in the mathematical sense precisely because they are digital; it is as if we have no way of studying the continuity of physical phenomena other than by approaching them with discontinuous analytical frameworks. It should be underscored that a nature populated by shortcuts between different scales—by emergence processes, or by "catastrophes" in the French mathematician René Thom's sense—could give the impression of a blurring of continuity and discontinuity. However, as with music that is recorded in the form of a discontinuous series of signals, the fact remains that while we systematically comprehend the world with discrete tools, we have never been so sensitive to the effects of continuity—to the very effects whose philosophical terms Deleuze set out to define.

The recent turn to digital discrete design pointed out by Carpo could very well represent an attempt to address this contradiction.[28] Architecture cannot, however, fully bridge the gap between the continuous nature on which it relies and the discontinuous digital tools that it uses, from computers to robots. Expressing contradictions is not solving them, especially since these contradictions are related to some of the deepest structures of the contemporary world.

A final tension must be acknowledged: the tension that exists between the desired amalgamation of matter with information or calculation (hence "material computation" as an idiomatic expression in design) and the actual disjunction between digital files and the matter that is informed by them (which is at the very source of computer-aided manufacturing). Digital culture aspires to see matter and information as fused together while at the same time systematically seeking to separate them. It is a culture that readily refers to the figure of the artisan working in close contact with materials, and often without any recourse to plans, in the manner of builders in the Middle Ages. Yet by the same token, it is a culture that relies on a radical disjunction between the file that holds the information and the matter that is shaped by the machine.

Regimes of materiality can be associated with particular forms of nostalgia. For instance, the intense admiration for ancient Roman technical prowess in the Renaissance and baroque periods prompted questions about whether it was possible for the moderns ever to surpass the ancients. Then, over the course of the long transition leading from the eclipse of the baroque age to the onset of the Industrial Revolution, there emerged two forms of anxiety, both tinged with regret. The first echoed resoundingly during the neoclassical period; it concerned the potential failure to recover the creativity, inspiration, and authenticity marking ancient Greek culture, which the German art historian Johann Winckelmann held up as the ultimate model in *Geschichte der Kunst des Alterthums (History of the Art of Antiquity)*, first published in 1764.[29] Perfect and at the same time lacking inner life, the works of

Italian sculptor Antonio Canova and Danish sculptor Bertel Thorvaldsen seem to illustrate this impossibility. Later, in the time of triumphant industrialism, the prospect of losing forever the spontaneous inspiration of the artisan's creative hand haunted the design world; in Britain, this fear, which was voiced in the works of John Ruskin, among others, rendered machine precision and the mass production of ornamentation questionable.[30]

As for the digital era, it extricates information from matter. It has separated the two in order to record information in series of zeros and ones that can be stored on all sorts of devices—regardless of their nature—before being reinjected into the physical world through the use of laser cutters and 3-D printers. It is fascinating how digital culture now voices regret over this state of affairs and dreams of mingling information and matter once again. Architects and designers have thus started to dream of restoring this lost unity. The figure of the artisan cherished by Ingold and Sennett surely has little in common with the one spiritualized by Ruskin. Yet by the virtue of its receptiveness to the forces that animate the physical world, digital culture is likely revealing a form of nostalgia that is linked to the sense that it is difficult to repair the rift between the information designers manipulate and the matter to which it is applied.[31]

To return specifically to architecture, it is striking that many of its current investigative paths are in tune with the new landscape broadly sketched out here. Proponents of the digital avant-garde readily refer to a continuous vision of nature, which is seemingly echoed by the smooth forms, cogenerating through inflections and folds, that they often design. Zaha Hadid was a master of this type of geometrical treatment, but it is also found in the work of many other architects, albeit expressed differently. Just as significant is the inspiration that the first architects following this trend claimed to have found in Deleuze's celebrated essay *Le Pli (The Fold)* (1988), thus epitomizing the link between their practice and a certain philosophical conception of the world.[32] There is certainly a resonance between some of the pursuits of contemporary architecture and the transformations that our notions of nature and materiality are currently undergoing.

Zaha Hadid Architects, Heydar Aliyev Center, Baku, Azerbaijan, 2012. Photograph by Aleksandr Zykov. Inflections and folds reign supreme in this signature building.

The digital avant-garde is concerned with themes such as the connections between living beings and algorithmic procedures. These constitute one of the experimental threads explored by the American architect Karl Chu, who has suggested that, in the future, buildings should be designed on the basis of algorithms that function like a sort of genetic code.[33] More broadly, these connections are also central to initiatives that claim to follow the precepts of material computation. Behind these experimental approaches, an alliance is repeatedly forming between organic inspiration and the use of algorithms; Marjan Colletti's and Michael Hansmeyer's designs are typical examples.[34] This leads to a reformulation of the long-standing question of animation, one calling at least as much on calculation as on the spontaneous empathy we feel when faced with certain material behaviors—as though

Michael Hansmeyer and Benjamin Dillenburger, Digital Grotesque I, 2013. Highly ornamental, this type of production epitomizes a challenge to the traditional frontier between the organic and the computational. It also raises the question of the subject that the "digital grotesque" ambitiously addresses.

calculation itself had now acquired the ability to generate the impression of spontaneity.

At the heart of the questions raised by contemporary architecture—and this goes well beyond the proposals of the digital avant-garde—lies an exploration of emergent configurations of materiality. This exploration is currently being carried out through means that are exclusive to the discipline of architecture and through the implicit or explicit calling into question of traditional concepts such as structure. The weakening of this latter concept, in particular, is accompanied by a characteristic indecisiveness regarding the scales at which architecture should operate. Numerous architects are thus testing models of material organization that are no longer as readable as traditional tectonic codes. The Beijing National Stadium (2008), designed by Herzog & de Meuron in collaboration with engineer Cecil Balmond, was conceived of as a network rather than as an articulated group of supported and supporting elements. Meanwhile, with projects such as the Zhengzhou Tower (2013) in China, Christian Kerez has been exploring configurations of posts and floors that call to mind the distribution of stems in a bamboo forest as opposed to traditional rows of columns.[35] Likewise in Kerez's work, the figure of the network seems to be superseding conventional forms of tectonic arrangement. The line of descent, which Papapetros suggests weds "the animation of the inorganic" (developed by certain strands of German art history and philosophy circa 1900) to the concept of animation prevalent today among digital architects, can be read in the light of this crisis of traditional tectonic arrangements.

Such a crisis also reflects the evolution of attitudes toward materials. With ever-increasing research on composite and smart materials as well as with manifold explorations of the possibilities opened up by the development of nanotechnologies, attention is, in many cases, turning toward the development of materials whose properties are defined in

Herzog & de Meuron, detail of the structure of the Beijing National Stadium, 2008. The structural and ornamental dimensions are difficult to distinguish in this realization presented by Cecil Balmond, its engineer, as an attempt to define an alternative tectonics based on "non-Cartesian" principles.

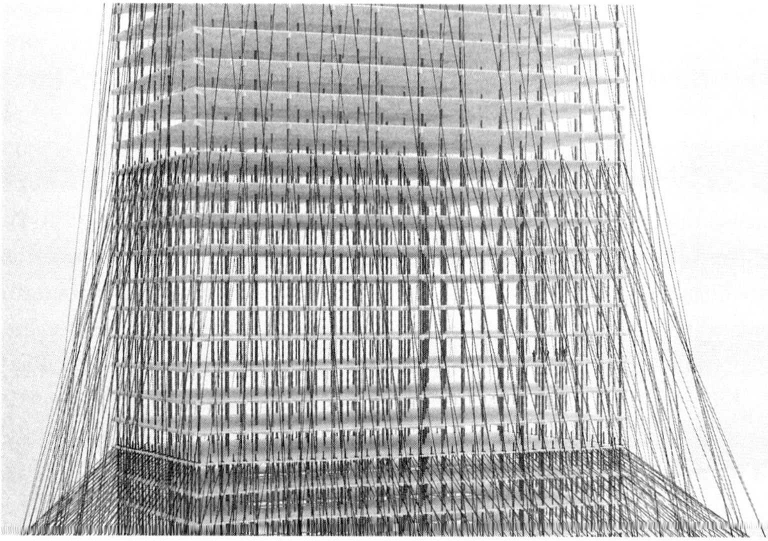

Christian Kerez, high-rise in Zhengzhou, China, 2013. Photograph by Milan Rohrer; copyright Christian Kerez. This is another project that blurs the distinction between the structural and the ornamental.

advance instead of toward the design of structures that fulfill functions that can be integrated into the very substance of matter.[36]

As architecture begins to turn its back on long-accepted structural ideals, it is abandoning a worldview in which the understanding of physical reality is based on the hypothesis that many things—from living creatures to buildings—are internally organized in ways that are distinct from their appearance. In the animal kingdom, the skeleton, invisible from the outside, used to be the most striking illustration of this hypothesis, and numerous architectural structures took inspiration from it. The importance accorded the skeleton went hand in hand with the favor that architecture accorded the scale of the body. This prerogative was undermined by the evolution of grandiose architectural programs—the proliferation of gargantuan buildings such as commercial centers and airports dwarfing the exhibition halls and railroad stations of the nineteenth century—as well as by design practices infused with a digital culture supported by zoom effects by means of which the very notion of scale became problematic.

It would seem, then, that in the course of a few decades designers have gone from a mind-set attentive to the skeletons of things to one fixated on the epidermis. This epidermis is complex and thick, in the material sense, precisely because of the mechanisms it must accommodate to fulfill our needs (ranging from energy efficiency to aesthetics). In this sense, architectural skins are unlimited by scale, able to envelop anything from a single pavilion to a gigantic commercial center. They are often textured and colored. In short, the crisis in structural thinking—the move from skeleton to skin—has been accompanied by a reinvention of ornament. This ornament, very different from that of the classical tradition, completely covers and, indeed, seems to mingle with the building's skin rather than being concentrated at the strategic points

Foreign Office Architects, John Lewis department store, Leicester, 2007. Photograph by Saturo Mishima; copyright Foreign Office Architects. Tactile or exerting a hypnotic effect, contemporary architectural ornament strongly suggests the abolition of the distinction between subject and object, as if both were actually immersed in the same affective continuum.

of its composition. It often possesses tactile or even hypnotic connotations, as with the spirals on the façade of the John Lewis department store in Leicester completed by Foreign Office Architects in 2007, and thereby seems to propose the abolition of the distinction between object and subject by plunging both into the same continuum of sensations and affects.[37]

The rise of an ornamental domain that plays with the effects of synesthesia—to see is to touch, to smell is to hear—and with the blurring of object and subject reflects a perception of the individual that is radically different from the one that the modern age sought to promote. The heroic body, dense and compact like the Statue of the Commander in Molière's play *Dom Juan* (1665), is being supplanted by a looser corporeality made up of networks and assemblages with hazy boundaries. In this context, ornament acts as an interface, or, to use a neuronal metaphor, as a synapse allowing the contemporary individual to exchange impulses with architecture. Nothing could be further removed from the quest for a formally articulated expression that characterized a whole array of architectural production at the end of the Enlightenment than our current search for a communicative mode premised on a direct connection between subject and building—a connection that ostensibly allows the two to exchange vague impressions and dreams rather than words.

Continuity, superficiality, hybridization, and connection as stand-ins for communication—these themes are ever present, informing everything from humans' perception of the obstinacy of things to their interpretation of who they actually are. In addition to this set of themes, which radically undermines traditional representations of the physical world and human beings, the digital age has revealed another rupture: the abandonment of the belief in the ontological difference between the unique object and the series, a series now enabled by digital design and fabrication through nearly infinite possibilities of variation from a single base model. This may have serious consequences for a discipline that hitherto knew only the isolated building or the prefabricated series, the two forms being considered mutually exclusive.[38]

In short, this set of transformations must be understood in relation to a massive shift in attitudes toward the physical world. The shift, which has led to a preference for collaboration (and not modernism's systematic recourse to violence with heroic overtones), is observable not only in relation to the use of digital methods. As much as the use of the computer as a design tool has spread, this shift also reflects the escalation of environmental concerns as well as the desire to preserve the world rather than transform it radically. In the architectural exploration of the new substance of materiality, the escalation of the environmental dimension is as critical as the digital realm. To return to structure, for example, its diminishment as a concept is inextricably linked to the shift from mechanics to thermodynamics as theorized by, among others, the Spanish architect Iñaki Abalos.[39] Indeed, the strategic character of questions related to the envelope reflects the rising importance of energy issues. On an even more basic level, at the point where the digital realm and efforts to achieve greater energy efficiency intersect, a whole range of phenomena are starting to take on a tangible character that they did not previously possess. This is the case with the temperature gradients, heat transfers, and humidity levels evident in the architect Philippe Rahm's work—these over and against the posts, beams, and concrete shells defining modern architecture.[40]

Under the joint effect of the digital realm and the quest for greater environmental efficiency, it is nonetheless possible for tectonics to be reinterpreted in terms other than the effectiveness of load paths and transfers; rather than playing the "smart envelope" card, for the regulation of the interior atmospheres of buildings some architects are putting their money on mass effects that allow energy to be stored and subsequently redistributed.[41] The transition from mechanics to thermodynamics, in other words, does not perforce condemn discussion of structure to an inexorable decline. To the contrary, it could lead to a different understanding of associated issues. Instead of an insistence on deciphering the "mechanical principles that govern all the phenomena of internal balance," as Torroja put it, emphasis would be placed on the interpretation of the terms of storage capacity and thermal exchange.[42]

Philippe Rahm architectes, Convective Building, IBA-Hamburg, 2010. Rahm's work illustrates the increasing importance of environmental factors in architecture: gradients of temperature, heat transfers, and levels of humidity are becoming as significant as structural considerations.

Where the spread of digital tools is concerned, the most radical impact on architecture is also the least visible, even if its effects can be felt far beyond discussions in neo-avant-garde circles. This concerns the status of design, or, more precisely, the forms that it takes. Traditionally, the design process was akin to a journey whose end point was a finalized compositional statement—a final form—that thereby was accorded special status. This final form appeared as a point of convergence—as an idea in the Platonic sense rendered gradually visible and unveiled at the end of an itinerary. Computers undermine this interpretation by making the final form of the design appear to be simply the result of a (sometimes arbitrary) choice from among a plethora of possible variations. Another way of envisioning this is to underscore that computers do not produce forms; rather, they produce families of forms—or “objectiles,” to borrow the term coined by Deleuze in reference to Bernard Cache’s work—or, even more simply, types of geometric and technical flux obtained through the variation of design parameters.[43] Consequently, the configuration selected by the architect can be compared to a sort of cut or freeze-frame.

In this scheme of things, it is not surprising to find that the nineteenth-century chronophotographic series produced by the French physiologist and scientist Étienne-Jules Marey and the English American photographer Eadweard Muybridge, in which animals and people are captured at different stages of single repetitive movements, hold such fascination for the first theorists of the digital, such as Lynn.[44] Like the moments caught by Marey and Muybridge, the final form of architectural design in the digital era would seem to possess a comparable status with regard to the geometric flux of which it constitutes a cut or selection. This cut is profoundly informational, in the sense that information refers precisely to the selection of a given state within a multitude of states in which a system might find itself. Again, an information bit is nothing other than an “atom of circumstance,” an elementary system in state zero or one. To be sure, parametric design is ultimately presented as a process of optimization that is meant to fight against the specter of arbitrariness in the final form. Yet the plethora of parameters that are taken into account prevents any particular solution from appearing absolutely superior to any other. Priorities always need to be set, and choices made, but it is difficult to pretend that arbitrariness is not somehow part of the adopted strategy.

The main consequence of this evolution is that architectural form no longer expresses the reassuring stability of what is; instead, it echoes the change that unfolds after a choice has been made, as an event that follows from an action. At the dawn of the computerization of architecture, Peter Eisenman glimpsed the imminence of this evolution with both his “iterative” projects (such as the Biozentrum in Frankfurt, designed in 1987) and “archaeological” projects (starting with Romeo and Juliet in 1985). Inspired by the processes of deconstruction Jacques Derrida had introduced in literary and philosophical analyses, Eisenman compared the architectural process to a series of procedures that leave traces situated beneath the metaphysical notion of presence.[45] In this way, he sought to undermine the architectural pretension of embodying completeness. There is no better antidote to technological determinism than to underscore how much architecture produced in the digital era owes to developments that began long before computers prevailed in professional firms. The digital realm appears less as a set of software and material tools than as a culture whose roots reach down far more deeply than the temporal layer that witnessed the development and use of computers and smartphones.

In this culture, form becomes performance—and we understand the many injunctions placed on it as being active instead of serving simply as a receptacle for the actions of others. These injunctions are at the core of what is sometimes called the "performalist" current in architecture.[46] From the moment when, through its modes of production, architecture joins the domain of actions that seek to become events, it is summoned to operate in the world no longer simply as a benevolent framework but instead as an actor in its own right. Such summoning can serve a variety of purposes, including improving the environment (as with energy-positive buildings), responding to societal challenges, and contributing to cultural debates. The development of interactive architectural environments, in which interactivity is dependent on the intensive use of sensors and other digital devices, falls well within this perspective.[47] The current trendiness of questions relating to architects' or even architecture's "agency"—the capacity to act—can be interpreted in this context.

Under the influence of a material world that appears to be fundamentally shaped by occurrences and events, architecture is gradually abandoning its traditional posture as an embodiment of the persistence of what exists. Instead, architecture is itself becoming an occurrence, an action, and an event. How else to interpret the rise of the globalized "star architecture" (or starchitecture) that spectacular architectural and urban events such as Frank Gehry's Guggenheim Museum in Bilbao (1997) have been proposing for nearly two decades? Even emergency architecture and urbanism come under the umbrella of this event-based regime, despite claims to the contrary embedded in humility and concerns about responding to the gravest of social, political, and environmental crises. Indeed, the rise of research on interactive environments and the possibility for architecture to take direct action, like a living organism, are part of this same regime. For now, in addition to form as event or as imported response to what is occurring on the ground, there is the building capable of recognizing, recording, and reacting to situations according to planned scenarios. With the development of sensors and decision-making algorithms, the smart house is becoming a reality. Will we eventually see interactive spaces that truly have voices, that exhibit the ability to converse with their occupants as in some science fiction movies? If this happens, one of the traditional boundaries of architectural animation will have been crossed in a definitive way. As for the substance of architectural design, it will gradually shift from the conception of spaces to that of occurrences and events made possible by the newfound capacity of the building itself to communicate and act.

It is worth speculating about the appropriateness of this event-based regime, or at least pondering whether its increasing hegemony should be contested, in the sense that the world also needs to recover some sort of serenity—to return to the calm that buildings have long represented in the face of the historical vicissitudes unfolding within and around them. Put another way, by seeking to emerge as an actor, architecture surely runs the risk of losing the power that it derived from its status as a container intended to give meaning to human presence. Are we pushing the architectural animation of matter too far and thereby falling into a potentially ineffective form of gesticulation? The event-based character that architectural form puts on display today should arguably be tempered by a rediscovery of the inertia that built masses still continue to set against it. More generally, questions need to be asked about the boundaries that should be imposed on the interactivity with which we are trying to invest certain spaces. While interactivity is, in theory, a positive aspect, one hopes that buildings will not overstep certain limits in their capacity to speak and to act. At stake is the potential transgression of the freedom of human will; the irritation we feel when a car crammed with electronics insistently reminds us to fasten our seat belts suggests that prudence is called for when we are faced with the temptation to endow the spaces we inhabit with too many mechanisms of control over, and intervention in, our lives.

Perhaps it is more useful to conceive of form as a catalyzer of situations rather than as an occurrence or event. This takes matters further than the "benevolent setting" proposed by Oleg Grabar, but not so far as to make architecture into an actor in its own right. While architecture is never merely a passive setting, it cannot ultimately be compared to an interactive machine (however much some have dreamed of this being so). In reality, architectural forms offer a compromise between the infinite diversity of potential uses and the excessive impositions that the propensity to speak or function in a specific way represents. In other words, architecture should suggest and orient rather than express itself in an authoritarian way such that dialogue is not possible anymore.

To conclude this chapter, I would like to return to the question of architecture's relation to language and to the tension that drives architecture to speak to people all the while recognizing the obstinacy of matter. Setting aside for the moment the radical view of buildings as becoming truly "smart," as talking directly to occupants, and as dictating human behavior in accordance with programmed interests, the question actually goes to the heart of how the symbolic dimension fits into the field of contemporary architecture. As mentioned previously, the history of architecture envisaged from the perspective of materiality reveals surprising analogies between historical episodes that otherwise seem to stand in complete contrast to each other. While digital architecture testifies to the potential dismantling of a certain number of fundamental presuppositions belonging to modernism, it nevertheless remains faithful to its distrustful attitude regarding the symbolic dimension—this despite the fact that the last decade has seen a marked return to ornament.

It is striking that the question of meaning has been jettisoned by many contemporary designers who, on the contrary, claim to have definitively dispensed with the need for symbolism. It is perhaps not so difficult to explain this attitude: on the one hand, it reflects a fear of falling prey to the kind of cheap and sleek denotations that characterized whole swaths of postmodernist design in the 1980s; on the other, it services a desire for efficiency whose ultimate aspiration is the production of an architecture that can be of greater use and relevance to the social and environmental situations facing the world today. By the same token, contemporary architecture—in particular, the digital avant-garde—seems to be reviving the modernist quest for a mode of architectural expression that is independent of language. This explains why any number of significant modern edifices—from Mies's Seagram Building (1958) to Gordon Bunshaft's Beinecke Library at Yale University (1963)—feature prominently in Farshid Moussavi and Michael Kubo's compendium *The Function of Ornament.*

This negative attitude, this need to reject the symbolic order of things, itself potentially fuels two equally dangerous tendencies. The first, perceptively outlined by Robert Levit in an essay on the return of ornament, consists in a reliance on the use of symbols that is not only unconscious but also, even more vexingly, bordering on the naive.[48] As the seventeenth-century French philosopher and scientist Blaise Pascal wrote in *Pensées (Thoughts)*: "Unfortunately, those who seek to become angels become beasts."[49] By seeking out an authenticity premised on the blanket rejection of linguistic connotation—by refusing to address the symbolic order and thereby preserve some measure of expressive possibility for the discipline—contemporary star architecture runs the risk of falling back on the very approach it attempts to denounce (if only because it must retain the support of clients who want their buildings to "speak" to a given public). The second tendency, which is less insidious but fundamentally more frightening, consists in rejecting symbolism in the name of elucidating objective bases for the discipline. Real-world challenges such as the need to respond to ever more exacting environmental regulations tend to promote unchecked positivist approaches. Urgent social and economic situations are doing this as well. How can the symbolic dimension remain relevant given the proliferation of shantytowns and refugee camps? If such a question rings hollow, it is because these are not mutually exclusive domains—and the rejection of the symbolic dimension becomes all the more difficult to fathom in a period marked by repeated attempts to give new meaning to our lives; religious fundamentalism and deep ecology are, after all, extreme forms of a largely universal quest for new and ancient wisdom to which countless publications have been dedicated.

Architecture certainly has a role to play in this quest. Indeed, it seems utterly self-destructive for so many designers to seek to deny the relevance of symbolism. In point of fact, the discipline of architecture cannot abandon expression (along with its inevitable linguistic nuances) without renouncing its claim to be distinct from the mere art of building. The latter question is still entirely topical, given the proliferation of soulless structures across the globe. The ultimate aim of architecture is not to save the world, but to help give it human meaning. This may not seem remarkable, but it is actually deeply significant. Let me be clear: this is not to advocate a stance marked by indifference toward the challenges the planet is facing. Instead, we need to keep intact the ambition that allowed the discipline of architecture to overcome its marginality in terms of cubic meters of cement poured annually in order to continue making itself heard in a built environment that mainly obeys the laws of globalized capitalism, as David Harvey and others insistently remind us.[50] That is to say, true usefulness and urgency, whether environmental or social, ultimately play a minor role when it comes to the pursuit of profit—and so restoring dignity and meaning to human interventions, as architecture seeks to do, thus proves crucial as an act of resistance.

Naive gesticulation on one side, the desire for uncompromising objectivity on the other—these are two equally dangerous obstacles looming over the path that architecture must follow so as to remain faithful to the ambition of animating matter without denying its obstinacy or fetishizing it. Yet recognizing the importance of the search for meaning is no panacea. Far from it, for we need to allow language to exert its powers of seduction and, at the same time, avoid succumbing to them. In architecture, meaning is never fixed or even organized according to rules comparable to those that organize syntax and vocabulary. To use a term that is dear to "new materialists," architecture stems more clearly from emergence, from an endless process of unveiling, than from the rather stable formulas governing linguistic structures.

To what realm does architecture belong? It is inseparable from matter but also from expression—on a road that leads to language yet remains separate from it by a distance that is impossible to bridge. Does this imply that architecture, in its intractable materiality, ultimately falls within the realm of geology as opposed to that of poetry? Replying in the affirmative would mean forgetting François Dagognet's helpful clarification: "The world of objects, which is immense, is in the end more revealing about the mind than the mind itself."[51] The intractable materiality of architecture does not preclude its deeply human essence. In the end, architecture responds to this profound question: What are we humans, given all the things around us that seem simultaneously impenetrable and yet strangely close to that which haunts our thoughts?

CONCLUSION

Situations and Décors

Toward a Politics of Architectural Materiality

Architecture does not aim to save the world, but it certainly seeks to improve it by ennobling relationships between people, as German neoclassical architect Karl Friedrich Schinkel famously declared.[1] How can architecture contribute to this betterment beyond the immediate satisfaction of its clients? In other words, how can the discipline be political? After a long eclipse following the end of modernism and the demise of its dream of a politically and socially progressive architecture, this question has made a spectacular return in the past decades.[2] By the same token, the issue of how architecture can be political has become a pressing one for theorists and historians. In this concluding essay, building on remarks made before, I would like to offer a few reflections on how the consideration of the materiality of architecture can enable an original approach to the relations between architecture and politics.

Until recently, the most common type of answer to the question of how architecture can be political involved a combination of two main lines of argument. First, buildings orient and, in some instances, even direct human behavior in ways that prove clearly political. Jeremy Bentham's panopticon, a prison layout that submits inmates to the gaze of an invisible watchman located in a central surveillance room, exemplifies this type of agency of the built environment. Second, and certainly not least, architecture reinforces the prevailing political order by expressing its core values through means ranging from compositional principles to ornamental vocabulary. An extreme but revealing case of this second type of political character is found in Albert Speer's monuments, which were designed to convey the ascendency of the Nazi regime to the German people. Practical agency and symbolic expression—these two types of responses of architecture to political agendas generally coexist. The Palace of Versailles, for instance, served the French absolute monarchy in a very concrete manner, through its overall spatial organization, by enforcing court rituals, as well as through its carefully staged décor that glorified the king's deeds.

The political relevance of architecture may be intentional, as in Speer's production and the Palace of Versailles, or it may be involuntary. Indeed, buildings may be determined by a political and social context without the conscious recognition of their designers. This is actually the most common case. Very often architects endorse political values and promote politically loaded practices without realizing it. Just as architecture is generally received by the public "in a state of distraction," as Walter Benjamin observed, its conception is often inadvertently political.[3]

In the past decade, a series of critiques have been raised against these received interpretations of the relations between architecture and politics. To begin with, architectural realizations often prove more ambiguous than their interpreters suppose. This is true also of numerous other built objects, particularly infrastructures, the political impacts of which are generally less straightforward than they may seem at first. There is perhaps no better example of this ambiguity than the impact of the notorious overpasses built by the New York twentieth-century master planner Robert Moses on the Long Island Parkway leading to Jones Beach, one of Moses's major realizations. Whereas American political scientist Langdon Winner has asserted, in a much-publicized analysis titled "Do Artifacts Have Politics?," that these bridges were designed with a low height to prevent poor people and black persons from accessing the recreation area in buses (which could not get under the arches), recent scholarship has shown that the evidence in this case is actually far from conclusive.[4] Ambiguities appear even more pronounced for buildings, which obey a much broader set of purposes and accommodate a wider range of practices.

The connections that theorists and historians of architecture tend to establish between the recourse to certain compositional and ornamental principles and political agendas are even more equivocal. For instance, in the 1930s, the quest for a new classical monumentality characterized regimes as different as those in the Soviet Union, Nazi Germany, and the United States. After World War II, the spread of modernism ignored the Iron Curtain division. In the light of these historical examples, Bruno Zevi's claim that modernist architecture, with its emphasis on asymmetry and even dissonance, is intrinsically more democratic than its Renaissance, baroque, and neoclassical counterparts, which privilege symmetry almost absolutely, appears wholly unfounded.[5]

Given the shortcomings of traditional analyses of the relations between architecture and politics, proponents of actor-network theory have proposed to depart from such approaches.[6] According to them, politics should no longer be defined in the usual sense of interactions between governments, politicians, parties, trade unions, and social movements; rather, it should be seen more as a global interplay that encompasses not only relations between humans but also the complex set of alliances and oppositions that humans form with all sorts of nonhuman entities, from natural phenomena and beings to artifacts and social constructs. Placed within such an enlarged frame, architects and buildings appear no longer as the only focus of study. They are to be analyzed within complex networks of actors that produce political effects. From such a perspective, politics does not affect architecture from the outside, as a preexisting sphere that exerts an influence on the built environment. It appears as a coproduction among a multiplicity of actors that includes designers, users, buildings, techniques, and architectural styles, as well as many other protagonists.

A similar departure from traditional analyses of the relations between architecture and politics has been advocated by the various affiliates of the Aggregate approach to the history of architecture and urban design. Instead of "actors," members of the Aggregate collaborative prefer to invoke “agencies,” but their aim is also to relocate architecture within a complex network of factors that contribute to the production of politics, or rather “governmentality,” a notion borrowed from Michel Foucault.[7]

Whereas the analyses of buildings and urban projects that they conduct are not always that different in practice from traditional studies, the proponents of these recent trends are seeking to disentangle their research from a history that, in their eyes, gave excessive privilege to designers and their realizations. By the same token, artistic intentionality tends to become a secondary problem, just like the degree of autonomy that the architectural discipline may actually possess when trying to address social and political issues. The question of how architects can be political as designers, and not only as skilled navigators on an ocean of often-contradictory factors, is no longer raised as such. In other words, the issue of what architecture can achieve by itself—not in complete isolation, of course, but as a discipline endowed with partly autonomous objectives and tools—is not really raised.

This oblivion appears all the more paradoxical given that architectural design has never before been invested with so many expectations regarding its political, social, and economic effects. In the eyes of various urban constituencies, from mayors to real estate developers, architecture is supposed to contribute to a better urban life, to make cities both more attractive and more sustainable. This background explains the development of “starchitecture,” with its trail of signature museums, high-rises, shopping malls, and airport terminals perceived as embodiments of a bright future. Following the success of Frank Gehry’s Guggenheim Museum in Bilbao, most cities now dream of buildings that can crystallize their hopes and give visibility to their strategies. In parallel, and often in relation with this first objective, sustainable projects attract a lot of attention today, attention that extends far beyond their actual impact on the metabolism of cities, as if, there again, architecture is particularly adept at conveying essential aspects of the urban future.

What can architecture achieve as a discipline? This concern explains my interest in two dimensions that are generally neglected by proponents of actor-network theory or Aggregate-like approaches to the history of architecture. The first involves the sensations that stem from the direct encounter with buildings. The experience of surface and volume, of space, texture, light, and color, exerts an influence on humans that often has political resonance beyond the individual character of the sensations thus aroused. When confronted by buildings, individuals respond in varied ways, but the architectural resources that buildings mobilize tend to generate certain sensations and affects that are related to the way humans think and act collectively. Take, for instance, the feelings conveyed by elementary sequences such as doors, staircases, and windows, or the impressions produced by changes in levels of illumination or by effects of opacity or transparency. These sensations and affects tend to function at a level that may appear as almost primitive, or in any case as anterior to the use of language. Think of the impression of authority conveyed by an elevated podium: the sense of physical and moral domination that it provides to whoever is standing on it seems to be rooted in experiences that predate most complex expressions of human civilization, beginning with speech and writing, as if the various hominids that came before modern humans had felt something similar simply by standing on boulders to stare down at their fellow creatures.

At the opposite end of the architectural spectrum, one finds symbolic intentions that have often been conveyed through complex ornamental systems. Because of their sophistication and their dependence on myths, histories of past events, and representations of natural and artificial patterns and objects—from rustication to geometric figures and from tree leaves to human tools and instruments—these symbolic intentions and the ornamental systems used to express them, at least until the rejection of ornament by modernist architecture, appear clearly as posterior to language. Besides affects, the symbolic and the ornamental constitute another dimension that I will explore in the quest for a renewed way to study the relations between architecture, envisaged as a partly autonomous discipline, and politics.

As noted previously, ornament has returned today under the influence of digital technology and a new longing for the pleasure it provides to the eye and mind. Paradoxically, this return has not generated a renewed interest among designers in the dimension of the symbolic in architecture. I will argue here that this dimension is unavoidable in architecture when one tries to address the issue of how architecture can be political. But this does not mean that one has to focus on the alleged correspondence between certain architectural resources, such as composition and style, and political agendas. Again, there is no univocal relation between them. Neither does such a return to the symbolic imply resurrecting the postmodern assimilation of ornament to language. Indeed, architectural ornaments are not comparable to words, nor décors to well-formed texts. They convey a longing for linguistic expression at the same time that they contribute to expressing the irreducibility of architecture to language through the role played by texture, color, and other material attributes in their constitution.

In the theory and history of architecture, the couple formed by the sensory and the symbolic has usually been mobilized by proponents of the phenomenological approach. They feature prominently in the work of one of the pioneers of this approach, Norwegian theorist and historian Christian Norberg-Schulz, as well as in the essays of Finnish architect Juhani Pallasmaa and the studies of ancient and early modern architecture of British historian Joseph Rykwert.[8] As always, phenomenologists have had a tendency to refer to an ahistorical conception of the sensory and the symbolic. Here, the association of these terms is envisaged in the historical terms provided by the study of the materiality of architecture. Materiality, as it has been defined in this book, contributes to the articulation of the sensory and the symbolic. As such, it plays an essential role in imparting architectural design with political relevance, and this beyond deterministic readings of architectural agency, whether this agency is understood in practical or symbolic terms.

Approaching the relations between architecture and politics from this perspective implies expanding the sphere of the political beyond the definitions usually retained by political science. Rather than the agendas promoted by social movements and organized parties, architecture deals with the ways in which collective human action can be framed so that it appears as meaningful. This framing mobilizes resources ranging from the capacity of surfaces, volumes, lights, and colors to create sensations and affects to the power of ornament to give pleasure and suggest significations.

From the sensory to the ornamental, the true political agency of architecture lies in two interrelated aspects. The first has to do with the capacity to generate situations that constitute incentives to orient action in certain directions. However, such orientation should not be confused with the deterministic effects traditionally attached to architectural organization by theorists, historians, and critics in their attempts to assess how architecture can be political. It works best through indirect hints, through the suggestions of possible collective meaning, rather than through the creation of definite constraints or the straightforward affirmation of certain values.

Inseparable from the generation of situations, one finds the power of architecture to create immersive environments that reinforce the feeling that human action can be meaningful. This is where ornament played a key role until its modernist demise. Beyond its explicit symbolic meaning, it constituted décors that enabled men and women to live in a world made commensurable with their fragile existence, a world that occupied an intermediary place between the transcendence of the divine and the immanence of nature, as Renaissance humanists Leon Battista Alberti and Daniele Barbaro suggested in their writings.[9]

This political agency is inseparable from the materiality of architecture envisaged as the specific way in which the architectural discipline contributes to the coproduction of the nonhuman and the human through sensations as well as symbols, through the generation of situations and the creation of décors. Such agency has more to do with making human action meaningful than with channeling it so that it meets with preexisting political agendas. What architecture does best is to invest human behavior with gravity—a notion where the physical meets the symbolic. Humans have still to decide in which direction this gravity may lead them. Contrary to Galileo's law of falling bodies, the experience of architecture is always multifaceted, open-ended, and ultimately ambiguous.

Let me begin with architectural sensations and the way they are conducive to the production of situations. The fundamental effectiveness of architecture lies in its capacity to organize matter in ways that provoke sensations and generate affects that can be widely shared. Many of those sensations and affects are created by means specific to the discipline, such as the definition of an outside and an inside, the play of scale and dimensions, and the contrast between light and shadow, or between opacity and transparency, to name only a few. Architecture can also contribute to focusing attention on specific areas—think of the pivotal role of the stage in theaters. The spatial resources of the discipline are usually mobilized in close connection with some key qualities of the materials employed, from brick to concrete and from wood to steel. Smoothness or roughness, grain, texture, and color constitute an integral part of architectural effects. These effects are seldom univocal. They are usually obtained through combinations of elements that may seem mutually exclusive. In many architectural realizations, the notions of outside and inside are both affirmed and challenged through their unlikely blend, while the distinction between light and shadow is often blurred. To the astonishment of the visitor, opposed characteristics merge. As historian of architecture Eve Blau has observed in an insightful article, architectural transparency is often obtained through the variation of degrees of opacity.[10] In order to make its basic operations more effective, architecture transforms them into complex moves, thickening its plot, so to speak, in ways that appear somewhat paradoxical. In addition to their inner complexity, architectural means and effects are often related to external factors such as urban locations and landscapes that give buildings their full power. At this level also, paradoxes abound, beginning with the capacity of architecture to be contextual through the seeming rejection of its immediate surroundings.

Following the phenomenologists, it is tempting to attribute to architectural sensations and affects immutable biological roots. After all, animals are sensitive to certain spatial effects, beginning with sharp contrasts in dimensions and light, as ethologist Temple Grandin has convincingly argued in books such as *Animals in Translation*.[11] Contemporary neuroscience tends to confirm this point of view. Some of the sensations and affects induced by spatial organization are definitely hardwired. From this perspective, the traditional assumption made by architectural theorists and philosophers that there is a primitive component at work in architecture, a component pointing toward the origins of humankind, appears plausible. Hegel was perhaps right in placing architecture at the dawn of the arts in his *Aesthetics*. Going further, there seems to be something as powerful as the first impressions of childhood in the sensations and affects produced by architecture.

This perspective is misleading, however, insofar as it tends to assimilate aspects as different as the animal-like, the primitive, and the childlike, an assimilation that has led in the past to all kinds of prejudiced discourses, such as those that associate non-Western societies and cultures with primitive and animal-like conditions. Above all, it should be recognized that most architectural effects are not reducible to mere biological phenomena. Indeed, they are complex in ways that bear the marks of society and culture. The manner in which Le Corbusier blurs the distinction between the outside and the inside in projects like the 1954 Mill Owners' Association Building in Ahmedabad, India, and the 1953 Casa Curutchet in La Plata, Argentina, is typical of a certain moment in the development of architectural modernism, a moment that is in turn representative of a broader postwar cultural context. Even more evident is the difference in the interpretation of transparency between a medieval masterpiece like the Sainte-Chapelle in Paris and Ludwig Mies van der Rohe's 1956 Crown Hall in Chicago. The former relies on stained glass to impart light with an almost supernatural character, while the latter mobilizes a more limited, seemingly objective, set of resources, beginning with the contrast between translucency and transparency proper.

The fact that architectural sensations and affects are to a large extent social constructs becomes even more evident if one pays attention to the way they are usually combined within larger ensembles that tend to propose perceptive and emotional itineraries, thus making possible what Le Corbusier called the "architectural promenade."[12] The concrete experience of architecture is rarely static. It unfolds in time as much as in space, a time saturated with cultural content, beginning with the tempos characteristic of a given society. There is, for instance, a strong link between the modernist conception of the architectural promenade and the mechanical and cinematic tempo of the twentieth century, just as medieval churches were meant for rhythms associated with a deeply religious vision and experience of the world.[13] I will return to this issue, for it represents an important component of architectural agency.

The biological dimension must not be neglected. It acts as a counterpoint to the tendency of culture to be overly constraining. Conversely, cultural content emancipates the subject in contact with the building from pure animal impulses. As a result, leaving aside extreme cases like Bentham's panopticon, architectural creations usually offer a mix of constraint and leeway. They appear as built situations inviting humans to act in certain directions.

Speaking of situations, how not to be reminded of the situationists and their interpretation of situations as constructs characterized by ambiances and a range of possible and at the same time surprising and even disruptive events that could unfold?[14] Less ambitious perhaps than the situationists and their desire to plan for the unexpected, architecture stages humans in certain ways, leaving them the opportunity to write the play, to decide which events will happen, who will be talking and who will remain silent, who will enter and who will exit, whether there will be a happy ending or a sad one.

To return to my earlier discussion of theatricality and the staging of human presence in the world: architecture favors certain configurations—such as the one in which we watch others perform a play in front of us as part of a designed setting—while seldom transforming these orientations into absolute necessities. At its core, the architectural discipline should not be confused with a kind of programmatic engineering. Answering the requirements of a brief does not make exhaustive use of the power of architecture (witness the significant differences that mark individual theaters as unique places): some stages are more conducive to comedy, others to tragedy, and there are theaters whose main function seems to be the promotion of a certain type of audience sociability. Charles Garnier's Paris opera house clearly belongs to the last category. In other words, architecture does not serve simply as a setting for our actions; it colors those actions in particular ways and can even suggest situations that will in some sense fulfill a deeper vocation.

Architecture defines a situation—that is, a built configuration—within which what is said and done matters. It provides an overall atmosphere and gives some scenic indications, but the plot remains undecided. At its best, when it creates the proper atmosphere, the discipline appears as an "ennobler of human relationships," to quote Schinkel again. One of the best-known engravings in Schinkel's collection of architectural designs shows a series of microevents made possible by the specific arrangement of the second-floor entrance to the 1828 Altes Museum in Berlin. A young man is commenting to a child—a younger brother or a son—on the meaning of one of the paintings that adorn this space. Two friends are walking along arm in arm, conversing. All these visitors have arrived by taking a staircase that has led them literally from shadow to light, thus preparing them for the proper appreciation of the works on display. The architecture insistently suggests that approaching art should require effort, and that the significance of art must be shared through human exchanges. In the distance, beyond the peristyle columns, we glimpse the city, the Prussian capital, whose cultural vocation the museum is designed to stimulate. The situation or the stage is undoubtedly political, without superfluous spatial and ornamental pathos. It clearly serves the ambitions of the Prussian state, but its message extends beyond the latter's quest for cultural legitimacy.

Often discrete, such staging is not to be confused with passivity, for architecture does indeed intervene through its capacity to close and open, to separate and unite, to lead from shadow to light, to make invisible or visible. All these operations can be political. Take invisibility versus visibility: it constitutes a means of action as powerful as enclosing or opening. An office building realized in 2012 by Rahul Mehrotra for the city of Hyderabad in southern India offers a brilliant demonstration of this power. The building uses a glass façade doubled by a vertical garden to create a visual relationship between strata of Indian society that usually ignore each other: the professional employees of a high-tech business that belongs to the higher castes and the

Karl Friedrich Schinkel, perspectival view from the upper entrance gallery of the Altes Museum in Berlin, from *Sammlung architectonischer Entwürfe,* 1819–40. This specific built situation revolves around the civilizing powers of artistic culture and the city.

near-untouchables who take care of watering and trimming the plants along the façade. Even if the building's various users are free to continue ignoring each other, architecture acquires a political significance through this sort of project, without falling into ideological demonstration. Chicago-based architect Jeanne Gang has also been working on the issue of mutual visibility in projects like her high-rise apartment tower Aqua (2009), where inhabitants can see each other from one balcony to another. There the challenge is not so much caste and class divide as it is the tendency of contemporary societies to promote anonymity and indifference. Perhaps the fashionable concept of "agency" should be reserved for this type of action: the creation of situations that can either reinforce or disrupt the usual dividing lines in society, starting with effects of visual and social distancing that make some people invisible to others. It could also be useful to mobilize at this stage the notion of "aesthetic regime" proposed by French philosopher Jacques Rancière to better approach what architecture ultimately does—whether it reinforces or, to the contrary, reorganizes "the distribution of the sensible," who and what can be seen, and by whom, in a given society.[15] Regimes of materiality have an evident link with Rancière's aesthetic regimes, since they involve vision as a social construct.

Architecture's agency, its capacity to generate situations, includes also the tempos that govern its assemblages of effects in relation to the prevailing rhythms of life. From Roland Barthes to Gilles Deleuze, and from Marc Bloch to Jean-Claude Schmitt, philosophers and historians, not to mention anthropologists, sociologists, and economists, have insisted on the political dimension of social rhythms.[16] The various ways collective time is organized, from production to worship, are indeed political insofar as they are constitutive of social relations. The

Rahul Mehrotra Architects, KMC Offices in Hyderabad, India, 2012. RMA Architects. Photograph by Carlos Chen. This architectural situation revolves around issues of mutual visibility between members of different Indian castes.

medieval social order, for instance, was inseparable from the rhythms imposed by religion on individuals, monastic communities, guilds, and cities. The development of industrial societies was inseparable from the new tempo imposed by mechanization. Chains of architectural sensations and affects contribute to these rhythms in specific ways. Romanesque and Gothic architecture was related to the social rhythms of the Middle Ages. In the 1920s and 1930s, Le Corbusier's desire to make architecture commensurable with the new speed of a mechanized society was more authentically political than his various attempts to seduce authoritarian regimes and their democratic counterparts.

After sensations and situations, let me turn to ornament and décor. For a very long time, ornamentation represented one of the most evident means through which architecture was connected to political questions. Ornaments displayed status, authority, and wealth. They expressed the actual ranks and the social aspirations of buildings' owners. Above all, they conveyed messages, thus participating in the communication strategies of empires, monarchies, aristocratic families, churches, religious orders, corporations, and guilds. Architectural ornaments were symbolic, and symbols were often political in character.[17]

In a good work of architecture, ornaments were not static elements distributed like signs on a sheet of paper. Rather, they appeared as markers in the process that enabled construction to become architectural, a process in many respects comparable to what today is called emergence. For a building to reveal itself as architectural was synonymous with a dynamic unfolding that mobilized ornaments to acquire visibility. From such a perspective, the main function of ornament was not to deliver explicit messages. Even if Greek temples and baroque churches were covered with statues, friezes, and low reliefs depicting mythological, religious, and historical scenes, ornaments were meant primarily to reveal the underlying order that made architecture possible.

I have chosen here to use the term *décor* to refer to the overall order produced by the coordination of ornaments; it is a convenient term, provided that one leaves aside the connotation of arbitrariness or even fakeness often associated with it. Etymology proves once more to be instructive here. *Décor* presents an evident connection with *decorum*, which refers to how individuals should behave according to circumstances. This relation suggests that traditional décor used to contribute, along with spatial effects, to the construction of architectural situations. It placed human action within an ordered frame that gave it both meaning and orientation. The responsibility of the plot was left to the actors, but the stage was set, and the play could start.

The symbolic content was more present with ornament and décor than with other architectural resources and effects. But here again, one must proceed with caution in examining how the symbolic and the impression of meaningfulness that it created were actually conveyed. Mythological stories and historical episodes, allegories, and emblems were only part of what enabled décor to contribute to the creation of a stage on which human actions mattered. Here also, one has to envisage the question from a dynamic perspective. Like traditional ornament, décor and its meaning must be understood as a process, a becoming meaningful rather than a once-and-for-all assigned signification. This dynamic character implies that the most profound signification of ornamented architecture, its true symbolic power, was never fully disclosed. It remained partly shrouded in mystery, like those episodes of our childhoods that we perceive as meaningful without fully realizing what they imply. Architecture used to evoke ideas of foundation not only because of the seemingly animal-like character of some of the sensations it aroused but also because of the persistent mystery that surrounded its symbolic content.

Contrary to the famous analogy drawn by Victor Hugo in *Notre-Dame de Paris,* architecture never really operated like a text. Despite its enduring fascination with writing, it was décor. Even more than instructive, monuments were supposed to be inspiring. For the inhabitants of medieval European cities, the signification of the ornamented façades of their cathedrals went far beyond the actual meanings of the scenes sculpted in stone. They spoke of common belief and hope, past the learned discourse of the clerics versed in the Old and New Testaments that guided the hands of craftsmen.

Beyond the details of religious and political agendas, architectural décor was able to convey emotions and values that reinforced the hold

Western façade of the Cathedral of Bourges at sunset. Photograph by Arnaud Frich. Contrary to what Victor Hugo famously suggested in *Notre-Dame de Paris*, medieval cathedrals probably functioned more as décor than as built books.

of these agendas on the people. This is how the abundant ornamentation of Versailles should be understood, past the ingenious allegories devised by the artists serving the Sun King. The exact meanings of these allegories were actually lost on many visitors to the palace, on the common men and women in particular, who did not have a sufficient stock of theological and literary knowledge to appreciate the subtle references to Christian dogma and Greco-Roman mythology that were spread over the walls and ceilings of the Great Apartments. Versailles nevertheless functioned as an efficient décor that added to the solemnity of the rituals of the monarchy and justified its pretensions to absolute rule.

Did we ever get rid of décor? Despite the modernist ban on ornament, the decorative dimension never totally lost its hold on architecture. In modernist architecture, objects, furniture, and textured and colored walls often played the role imparted to ornament until the dawn of the twentieth century.[18] There is no architectural situation without something like décor that extends the sheer power of surfaces, volumes, and lights. With the return of the ornamental today, this complementarity between situation and décor is again becoming evident. What is less understandable, however, is the refusal of so many designers to acknowledge the unavoidably symbolic aspect of their production. This refusal is at least as problematic as its opposite, the acceptance of heavily ideological ornaments and décors at times when nobody thought to challenge the necessity for architecture to convey meaning, such as throughout the nineteenth century, when allegories of churches, nations, and institutions, as well as of their virtues, multiplied outside and inside public buildings. In many cases, such denial corresponds to assent in disguise, an approval of the way the world is currently run, with its ruthless capitalistic principles and its increasing inequality between social groups. "Starchitecture," as well as the various neo-avant-gardes that strive to achieve recognition in its wake, accepts a political and social order in which competition, be it economic or artistic, has become the almost exclusive guideline. In other words, the temptation displayed by a large part of contemporary architecture to be an objective marker of the condition in which it is produced must be challenged insofar as it denies the very possibility of critical thinking and the perspective of an alternative to boundless capitalism.

The architectural discipline orders matter to create situations and their related décors. As expressions of the materiality of architecture, situations and décors also tell humans something about who they think they are. Although other practices, from painting and sculpture to the culinary arts, have to do with the issue of the tangible and its relation to subjectivity, architecture occupies a special position insofar as humans inhabit it. To inhabit means precisely to lead one's life and structure one's subjectivity in direct relation with tangible elements such as floors, walls, doors, and windows. Moreover, inhabiting or dwelling enables humans to establish relations with their fellow humans and, above all, stabilize them. This is where the true political power of architecture lies.

As I indicated at the beginning of this Conclusion, my ambition is to deal with the question of politics in relation to the specific resources of architecture—in other words, to show how architecture, envisaged as a partially autonomous discipline, can be political. Paradoxically, since it is inseparable from a broad cultural context ranging from the socially constructed everyday experience of things to the available science and technology, materiality enables the fulfillment of this agenda. In architecture, autonomy often expresses itself through the connections of the discipline to the society that produces it. Pure formalism is seldom the best path toward disciplinary identity, nor, for that matter, is the reduction of design to a series of practical solutions to programmatic needs. This double distance from disciplinary solipsism and overcontextualization translates into the capacity of buildings to withstand the test of time and continue to move visitors from later ages. Architecture seems all the more likely to address new generations of visitors when it does not refer only to itself or appear as a mere spatial translation of long-gone uses.

The outline of a history of architecture from the perspective of the changing regimes of materiality that I have sketched in this book may also be read as a history of the successive interpretations of the political fostered by the architectural discipline. For example, Renaissance architecture is inseparable from a shift in the understanding of the tangible world, a world perceived as fundamentally ordered, measurable, and proportioned, hence the possibility of representing it in plan, elevation, and perspective. This evolution is also linked to the new interpretation of the subject proposed by humanism. Order, measure, and proportion: these fundamental features of the new materiality that Renaissance architecture contributes to exploring through its regular compositions, which appeal to the perspectival perception of the humanist subject, present evident connections with the rise of the political ideal of rational government. Good government becomes synonymous with the determination of the proper balance between constituencies and their respective forces, a rational conception formulated by, among others, Niccolò Machiavelli. The politics of Renaissance architecture, as expressed through the investigation of a new form of materiality, thus extends beyond its role as servant of the specific ambitions of popes, bishops, kings, and other rulers.

The politics of materiality is of course not limited to this type of major transition between regimes of materiality. It expresses itself at multiple other moments, through the attempts made by designers to inflect the codes that prevail in the societies in which they live. Such a perspective enables us to throw a more accurate light on the contribution of architects like Albert Speer to totalitarian regimes. Beyond the effects produced by their neoclassical compositions and their symbolic use of eagles and swastikas, Speer's buildings appear as proposals regarding the relations between the material world and human subjectivity. They enroll concrete and stone, light and darkness, in a complex game meant to exalt the raw forces of a telluric nature miraculously aligned with cutting-edge militaristic technology. This game was designed to elevate certain subjects—the Führer, the Nazi high dignitaries, and key groups, from elite troops to German athletes—while belittling others, beginning with the common people in isolation, who were meant to experience at the same time the formidable power of the Nazi Party and their own insignificance. Techniques such as the use of dimensions dwarfing the human body for certain architectural elements were mobilized for this purpose, as was the decorative power of Nazi ornaments.

From this standpoint, the rejection of modernist architecture by the totalitarian regimes of the first half of the twentieth century (leaving aside famous and rare exceptions such as Giuseppe Terragni's 1936 Casa del Fascio in Como, Italy) becomes easier to understand. For totalitarian regimes such as German Nazism and Italian Fascism, the materiality of architecture was inseparable from the project of exalting certain individuals and groups while belittling all the others. Despite their recurring reference to a mythical and supposedly inclusive People, these regimes mobilized the discipline to assert differences in dignity between humans. While not necessarily egalitarian, modernist architects had the ambition to treat everyone with equal dignity. Nothing is more telling in that respect than the Gardener's House of the Villa Savoye. Le Corbusier designed this modest-sized house with the same concern for architectural elegance that he devoted to the villa, which was intended for wealthy clients. Treating everyone with dignity, whatever their social standing, was a key modernist concern, a concern that today still inspires projects such as Mehrotra's Hyderabad office building.

The materiality of architecture does not guarantee that the resources of the discipline will be mobilized for good purposes only. Speer was not the first designer to use architectural resources for wrong causes. As for modernist architects, while they strove to treat everyone with dignity, they failed in their attempts to create a perfect world through efficient planning and good design. Given the pressing social and political challenges of the first half of the twenty-first century, the fundamental ambiguities and limitations of the architectural discipline may seem frustrating. But they are also synonymous with the possibility for architecture to remain autonomous as well as to produce specific results by allowing human actions literally to take place. Without agoras, forums, assembly rooms, and parliament chambers, and without their symbols and décors, a concept as abstract as democracy would not have known the same success. No politics are possible without the situatedness and embodiment that built situations and décors enhance. In the age of the Internet and online exchanges, the materiality of architecture still appears as a cornerstone of politics. It whispers in our ears that political decisions should still be made by the embodied animals that we call humans.

Acknowledgments

The project of this book emerged at the intersection of a series of enduring interests of mine, such as the relations among architecture, construction, and culture, and the strong connection between digital architecture and questions pertaining to matter and materiality. Ornament and its past and current role in architecture are also very present, often in conjunction with the recurring attempts of architecture to "speak." I hope that my reader will forgive my numerous references to Le Corbusier. They were difficult to avoid, given that I chair the foundation that bears his name.

Simultaneously, *The Materiality of Architecture* owes much to a number of intellectual encounters and conversations. Laurent Baridon's interest in the subject was important at the start of the project. Sarah Whiting, Lucia Allais, and Martin Bressani read the manuscript closely at different stages; the final result is indebted to their penetrating remarks and critiques.

The support of my editor, Pieter Martin, has proved essential. Abigail Grater has been, as always, a rigorous and creative translator.

I thank the colleagues and friends who graciously granted me rights to reproduce images from their work in the book: Fabio Gramazio and Matthias Kohler, Michael Hansmeyer, Christian Kerez, Rahul Mehrotra, Farshid Moussavi, Philippe Rahm, Gilles Retsin, and Lars Spuybroek.

Brigitte Bouvier and Arnaud Dercelles helped me find illustrations from the rich Fondation Le Corbusier archive.

My primary debt is to my Harvard friend and colleague Erika Naginski, without whom the final English version of this book, considerably revised and expanded from the French, would not have happened. I cannot thank her enough for her incisive mind and intellectual generosity.

Notes

Introduction

1. Around the fiftieth anniversary of Le Corbusier's death, controversy arose over the general interpretation of the architect's output, revealing ongoing major reservations regarding his work. See in particular François Chaslin, *Un Corbusier* (Paris: Le Seuil, 2015).

2. On Vitruvius and his treatise, see Pierre Gros, *Vitruve et la tradition des traités d'architecture: Fabrica et ratiocinatio* (Rome: École Française de Rome, 2006).

3. Mohsen Mostafavi and David Leatherbarrow, *On Weathering: The Life of Buildings in Time* (Cambridge: MIT Press, 1993).

4. Georg Simmel, "The Ruin," in *Essays on Sociology, Philosophy and Aesthetics*, ed. K. H. Wolff (New York: Harper & Row, 1965), 259–66.

5. Tim Ingold, *Making: Anthropology, Archaeology, Art and Architecture* (London: Routledge, 2013).

6. John Ruskin, *The Seven Lamps of Architecture* (London: Smith, Elder, 1849); Richard Sennett, *The Craftsman* (New Haven, Conn.: Yale University Press, 2009); Ingold, *Making*.

7. Walter Benjamin, "The Work of Art in the Age of Its Technological Reproducibility" (1936), trans. Howard Eiland, in *Selected Writings*, vol. 3, *1935–1938*, ed. Howard Eiland and Michael W. Jennings (Cambridge, Mass.: Harvard University Press, 2002), 101–33, esp. 119–20.

8. Oleg Grabar, *The Mediation of Ornament* (Princeton, N.J.: Princeton University Press, 1992), 193.

9. Louis Kahn, *Writings, Lectures, Interviews* (New York: Rizzoli, 1991), 76.

10. Nicolas Le Camus de Mézières, *The Genius of Architecture; or, The Analogy of That Art with Our Sensations* [*Le Génie de l'architecture, ou, L'Analogie de cet art avec nos sensations*, 1780], trans. David Britt (Santa Monica, Calif.: Getty Center for the History of Art and the Humanities, 1992), 70–71. On the theory of character, see also Werner Szambien, *Symétrie, goût, caractère: Théorie et terminologie de l'architecture à l'âge classique 1500–1800* (Paris: Picard, 1986).

11. Albert Camus, *The Myth of Sisyphus* [*Le Mythe de Sisyph*, 1942], trans. Justin O'Brien (London: Penguin, 2013).

12. On this concept, see Spyros Papapetros, *On the Animation of the Inorganic: Art, Architecture, and the Extension of Life* (Chicago: University of Chicago Press, 2012).

13. Descartes's conception of matter is exposed for instance in his treatise *The World (Le Monde, ou Traité de la lumière et des autres principaux objets des sens)*, published for the first time in 1664.

14. Jean-Paul Sartre, *Nausea* [*La Nausée*, 1938], trans. Lloyd Alexander (New York: New Directions, 1964).

15. An abundant literature is devoted to the history of modern concrete and the progressive definition of its properties. See, for instance, Cyrille Simonnet, *Le Béton, histoire d'un matériau: Économie, technique, architecture* (Marseille: Editions Parenthèses, 2005); Adrian Forty, *Concrete and Culture: A Material History* (London: Reaktion Books, 2012).

16. Martin Heidegger, "Building Dwelling Thinking" (1954), in *Poetry, Language, Thought*, trans. Alfred Hofstadter (New York: Harper & Row, 1971), 145–61. I use the term *dwelling* here in a more narrowly architectural and urban sense than does Heidegger, although inhabiting a place or a building and dwelling on earth are actually connected, as Heidegger points out.

17. Thomas Kuhn, *The Structure of Scientific Revolutions* (Chicago: University of Chicago Press, 1962).

18. Stephen Kern, *The Culture of Time and Space, 1880–1918* (Cambridge, Mass.: Harvard University Press, 1983).

19. François Hartog, *Regimes of Historicity: Presentism and Experiences of Time* [*Régimes d'historicité: Présentisme et expérience du temps*, 2003], trans. Saskia Brown (New York: Columbia University Press, 2015).

20. Kenneth Frampton, *Studies in Tectonic Culture: The Poetics of Construction in Nineteenth and Twentieth Century Architecture* (Cambridge: MIT Press, 1995).

21. I have developed this theme in some of my earlier writings, including "Architecture and the Virtual: Towards a New Materiality," *Praxis: Journal of Writing + Building*, no. 6 (2004): 114–21; and especially *Digital Culture in Architecture: An Introduction for the Design Professions* (Basel: Birkhäuser, 2010).

22. Lars Spuybroek, *The Sympathy of Things: Ruskin and the Ecology of Design* (Rotterdam: V2, 2011).

23. Juhani Pallasmaa, *The Eyes of the Skin: Architecture and the Senses* (Chichester: John Wiley, 2005).

24. Bruno Latour, *Reassembling the Social: An Introduction to Actor-Network-Theory* (New York: Oxford University Press, 2005).

25. Annick Jaulin and Refik Güremen, eds., *Aristote, l'animal politique* (Paris: Éditions de la Sorbonne, 2017).

26. On the "new materialism," see Diana Coole and Samantha Frost, eds., *New Materialisms: Ontology, Agency, and Politics* (Durham, N.C.: Duke University Press, 2010). For comprehensive overviews of actor-network theory and object-oriented ontology approaches, see Latour, *Reassembling the Social;* Graham Harman, *Object-Oriented Ontology: A New Theory of Everything* (London: Pelican Books, 2018).

27. The British theorist and anthropologist Albena Yaneva offers a remarkable example of the use of actor-network theory in the field of architecture in books like *Mapping Controversies in Architecture* (Burlington, Vt.: Ashgate, 2012). Beyond this type of direct influence, interest in techniques and in the agency of things and objects ranks highly among the concerns of the members of the American architectural history collaborative known as Aggregate. For an overview of their positions, see Aggregate, *Governing by Design: Architecture, Economy, and Politics in the Twentieth Century* (Pittsburgh: University of Pittsburgh Press, 2012). For a more recent picture of the research projects conducted under this group's umbrella, see the Aggregate online platform, accessed July 7, 2019, http://we-aggregate.org.

28. Michelle Addington and Daniel Schodek, *Smart Materials and New Technologies for the Architecture and Design Professions* (Oxford: Architectural Press, 2005).

29. Thomas Schröpfer, ed., *Material Design: Informing Architecture by Materiality* (Basel: Birkhäuser, 2011).

30. The influence of Deleuze was especially noticeable in the early years of digital architecture. See Mario Carpo, "Ten Years of Folding," in *Folding in Architecture,* ed. Greg Lynn, rev. ed. (Chichester: John Wiley, 2004), 14–19.

31. Achim Menges, ed., "Material Computation: Higher Integration in Morphogenetic Design," special issue, *Architectural Design* 82, no. 2 (March–April 2012); Jenny E. Sabin and Peter Lloyd Jones, *LabStudio: Design Research between Architecture and Biology* (New York: Routledge, 2018).

32. Frampton, *Studies in Tectonic Culture.* In this book, Frampton set out to restore the tectonic dimension of modern architecture over and against digital architecture, which he saw as divorced from any authentic material grounding.

33. This is the case with artists such as Richard Serra and James Carpenter. Carpenter's work in particular blurs the distinction between art and architecture. Sandro Marpillero, *James Carpenter: Environmental Refractions* (Basel: Birkhäuser, 2006).

34. Hartog, *Regimes of Historicity.*

35. Ingold, *Making.*

36. Andrew Cole, "The Call of Things: A Critique of Object-Oriented Ontologies," *Minnesota Review,* no. 80 (2013): 106–18.

1. From Making to Expression

1. See Georg Wilhelm Friedrich Hegel, *Introductory Lectures on Aesthetics* [*Vorlesungen über die Ästhetik,* 1818–29], trans. Bernard Bosanquet (Harmondsworth: Penguin, 1993).

2. François Blondel, *L'Art de jetter les bombes* (Paris: Author and N. Langlois, 1683).

3. Vitruvius drew the distinction between *fabrica* and *ratiocinatio*: the fabrication or practice of architecture and a more speculative dimension that critics typically assimilate with theory.

4. See, for example, Hanno Walter Kruft, *A History of Architectural Theory: From Vitruvius to the Present* [*Geschichte der Architekturtheorie: Vonder Antike bis zur Gegenwart,* 1985], trans. Ronald Taylor, Elsie Callander, and Antony Wood (New York: Princeton Architectural Press, 1994); Georg Germann, *Einführung in die Geschichte der Architekturtheorie* (Darmstadt: Wissenschaftliche Buchgesellschaft, 1987).

5. Antoine Picon, *French Architects and Engineers in the Age of Enlightenment* [*Architectes et ingénieurs au siècle des Lumières,* 1988], trans. Martin Thom (Cambridge: Cambridge University Press, 1992).

6. Joseph Rykwert, *On Adam's House in Paradise: The Idea of the Primitive Hut in Architectural History* (New York: Museum of Modern Art, 1972).

7. Le Corbusier, *Œuvre complète 1938–1946* (Zurich: Artemis, 1946), 170: "rend compliqué le mal et simple le bien."

8. Structure or tectonics? Kenneth Frampton uses both terms in *Studies in Tectonic Culture,* which sometimes leads to confusion. I would argue that tectonics, a notion mainly employed by German theorists in the nineteenth century, starting with Gottfried Semper, involves two distinct ideas: that of a structure that is formed through the assembly or weaving together of elements, and that of an architectural space that is in some sense generated by structural order. It is the latter idea that Frampton mainly holds in his book. A panorama of the possible interpretations of tectonics can be found in Isak Worre Foged and Marie Frier Hvejsel, eds., *Tectonics in Architecture: Reader* (Aalborg: Aalborg University Press, 2018).

9. Joseph Rykwert, *The First Moderns: The Architects of the Eighteenth Century* (Cambridge: MIT Press, 1980).

10. On this subject, see Antoine Picon, "The Freestanding Column in Eighteenth-Century Religious Architecture," in *Things That Talk: Object Lessons from Art and Science*, ed. Lorraine Daston (New York: Zone Books, 2004), 67–99.

11. See Michael Petzet, *Soufflots Sainte-Geneviève und der französische Kirchenbau des 18. Jahrunderts* (Berlin: Walter de Gruyter, 1961), 147.

12. David E. Nye, *American Technological Sublime* (Cambridge: MIT Press, 1994).

13. Peter Eisenman, "Aspects of Modernism: Maison Dom-Ino and the Self-Referential Sign," *Oppositions* 15/16 (Winter/Spring 1979): 118–28.

14. Heinrich von Kleist, *Correspondance complète 1793–1811*, trans. Jean-Claude Schneider (Paris: Gallimard, 1976), 136.

15. Michèle Cohen-Halimi, *Entendre raison: Essai sur la philosophie pratique de Kant* (Paris: J. Vrin, 2004), 73–74.

16. Charles Perrault, *Pensées chrétiennes de Charles Perrault*, ed. Jacques Barchilon and Catherine Velay-Vallantin (Paris: Papers on French Seventeenth Century Literature, 1987), 55–56, from *Pensées chrétiennes et pensées morales, physiques, métaphysiques et autres qui regardent la philosophie*, 1694–1703, Ms F 25575, Bibliothèque Nationale de France.

17. Michel Foucault, *The Order of Things: An Archaeology of the Human Sciences* [*Les Mots et les choses: Une archéologie des sciences humaines*, 1966], trans. Alan Sheridan (New York: Pantheon, 1970); Michel Foucault, *The Archaeology of Knowledge* [*L'Archéologie du savoir*, 1969], trans. A. M. Sheridan Smith (London: Tavistock, 1972).

18. Eugène-Emmanuel Viollet-le-Duc, *Discourses on Architecture* [*Entretiens sur l'architecture*, 1863–72], trans. Henry van Brunt (Boston: James R. Osgood, 1875), 1:56. On Viollet-le-Duc's theoretical concepts, see Jean-Michel Leniaud, *Viollet-le-Duc ou les délires du système* (Paris: Mengès, 1994); Laurent Baridon, *L'Imaginaire scientifique de Viollet-le-Duc* (Paris: L'Harmattan, 1996); Martin Bressani, *Architecture and the Historical Imagination: Eugène-Emmanuel Viollet-le-Duc, 1874–1879* (Burlington, Vt.: Ashgate, 2014).

19. Eugène-Emmanuel Viollet-le-Duc, *Dictionnaire raisonné de l'architecture française du XIe au XVIe siècle* (Paris: B. Bance, A. Morel, 1854–68).

20. Viollet-le-Duc, *Discourses on Architecture*, 74.

21. Erwin Panofsky, *Gothic Architecture and Scholasticism* (Latrobe, Pa.: Archabbey Press, 1951).

22. Heinrich Wölfflin, *Prolegomena to a Psychology of Architecture* [*Prolegomena zu einer Psychologie der Architektur*, 1886], trans. Harry Francis Mallgrave and Eleftherios Ikonomou, in *Empathy, Form, and Space: Problems in German*

Aesthetics, 1873–1893, ed. Harry Francis Mallgrave and Eleftherios Ikonomou (Santa Monica, Calif.: Getty Center for the History of Art and the Humanities, 1994), 149–87.

23. Eduardo Torroja, *Les Structures architecturales: Leur conception, leur réalisation* [*Razón y ser de los tipos estructurales*, 1960], trans. Albert Chaulet (Paris: Eyrolles, 1971), 28.

24. Alberto Pérez-Gómez, *Architecture and the Crisis of Modern Science* (Cambridge: MIT Press, 1983); Pallasmaa, *Eyes of the Skin.*

25. See Neil Leach, David Turnbull, and Chris Williams, eds., *Digital Tectonics* (Chichester: John Wiley, 2004); Cecil Balmond, *Informal* (Munich: Prestel, 2002).

26. I discuss the links between the crisis in tectonics and the rise of the digital realm in *Digital Culture in Architecture.*

27. On the theme of transhumanism and posthumanism, see Katherine N. Hayles, *How We Became Posthuman: Virtual Bodies in Cybernetics, Literature, and Informatics* (Chicago: University of Chicago Press, 1999); Céline Lafontaine, *L'Empire cybernétique: Des machines à penser à la pensée machine* (Paris: Le Seuil, 2004).

28. Laurent Baridon, "Le Mythe de Dinocrate: L'Architecte, le corps et l'utopie" (original typescript presented for HDR [accreditation to supervise research] at the Université de Paris I Panthéon-Sorbonne, 2005).

2. Architecture and Language

1. On the notion of "speaking architecture" at the end of the eighteenth century, see Anthony Vidler, *The Writing of the Walls: Architectural Theory in the Late Enlightenment* (New York: Princeton Architectural Press, 1987). See also Nicolas Molok, "'L'Architecture parlante,' ou Ledoux vu par les romantiques," *Romantisme*, no. 92 (1996): 43–53.

2. John Summerson, *The Classical Language of Architecture* (London: British Broadcasting Corporation, 1963).

3. Bruno Zevi, *The Modern Language of Architecture* [*Il linguaggio moderno dell'architettura*, 1973] (Seattle: University of Washington Press, 1978), 3.

4. Jesse Reiser and Nakano Umemoto, *Atlas of Novel Tectonics* (New York: Princeton Architectural Press, 2006), 172–73.

5. Farshid Moussavi and Michael Kubo, eds., *The Function of Ornament* (Cambridge, Mass.: Harvard Graduate School of Design, 2008).

6. Robert Venturi, Denise Scott Brown, and Steven Izenour, *Learning from Las Vegas* (Cambridge: MIT Press, 1972), 100.

7. Jacques Derrida, *Of Grammatology* [*De la grammatologie*, 1967], trans. Gayatri Chakravorty Spivak (Baltimore: Johns Hopkins University Press, 1998).

8. Françoise Choay, *The Invention of the Historic Monument* [*L'Allégorie du patrimoine*, 1992], trans. Lauren M. O'Connell (Cambridge: Cambridge University Press, 1999).

9. Victor Hugo, *The Hunchback of Notre Dame* [*Notre-Dame de Paris*, 1831] (Ware, Herefordshire: Wordsworth Classics, 1993), 153.

10. Quoted in Molok, "'L'Architecture parlante,'" 53. See also Barry Bergdoll, *Léon Vaudoyer: Historicism in the Age of Industry* (Cambridge: MIT Press, 1994).

11. On this subject, see Jean-Marie Pérouse de Montclos, *Étienne-Louis Boullée* (Paris: Flammarion, 1994).

12. Antoine Picon, *Ornament: The Politics of Architecture and Subjectivity* (Chichester: John Wiley, 2013).

13. Nigel Llewellyn, "Two Notes on Diego da Sagredo," *Journal of the Warburg and Courtauld Institutes* 40 (1977): 292–300.

14. On this work, see John Wilton-Ely, introduction to *Observations on the Letter of Monsieur Mariette: With Opinions on Architecture, and a Preface to a New Treatise on the Introduction and Progress of the Fine Arts in Europe in Ancient Times* [1765], by Giovanni Battista Piranesi, trans. Caroline Beamish and David Britt (Los Angeles: Getty Research Institute, 2002), 1–83. See also William Rieder, "Piranesi's Diverse Maniere," *Burlington Magazine* 115, no. 842 (May 1973): 308–17; Erika Naginski, "Preliminary Thoughts on Piranesi and Vico," *RES: Anthropology and Aesthetics*, nos. 53/54 (Summer/Fall 2008): 150–65.

15. Valérie Nègre, *L'Ornement en série: Architecture, terre cuite et carton-pierre* (Brussels: Mardaga, 2006).

16. Adolf Loos, *Ornament and Crime* [*Ornement und Verbrechen*, 1908], trans. Michael Mitchell (Riverside, Calif.: Ariadne Press, 1998).

17. On the "return" of ornament, see Moussavi and Kubo, *Function of Ornament*; Robert Levit, "Contemporary 'Ornament': The Return of the Symbolic Repressed," *Harvard Design Magazine*, no. 28 (Spring/Summer 2008): 70–85; Picon, *Ornament*.

18. Cole, "Call of Things," 107–8.

3. Animation and Materiality

1. Peter E. Knox and J. C. McKeown, eds., *The Oxford Anthology of Roman Literature* (Oxford: Oxford University Press, 2013), 249.

2. See, for example, Rudolf Wittkower, "The Problem of Harmonic Proportion in Architecture," in *Architectural Principles in the Age of Humanism* (New York: W. W. Norton, 1971), 101–54.

3. See François Duchesneau, *Les Modèles du vivant de Descartes à Leibniz* (Paris: Vrin, 1988).

4. Rory Cellan-Jones, "Stephen Hawking Warns Artificial Intelligence Could End Mankind," BBC News, December 2, 2014, http://www.bbc.com/news.

5. Pierre Caye, *Empire et décor: La Question de la technique à l'âge humaniste et classique* (Paris: Vrin, 1999).

6. Picon, *Ornament,* 124.

7. Gershom Scholem, *Major Trends in Jewish Mysticism* (Jerusalem: Schocken, 1941).

8. Lucy Bullivant, ed., *Responsive Environments: Architecture, Art and Design* (London: Victoria and Albert Museum, 2006).

9. Torroja, *Les Structures architecturales,* 28. In his book *On the Animation of the Inorganic,* Spyros Papapetros favors this psychological dimension, which was prominent in German philosophy and art history in the years around 1900.

10. On the role played by the notion of empathy in German philosophy and art history in the years around 1900, see in particular Harry Francis Mallgrave and Eleftherios Ikonomou, eds., *Empathy, Form, and Space: Problems in German Aesthetics, 1873–1893* (Los Angeles: Getty Center for the History of Art and the Humanities, 1994). On the far less well-known French attempts to explain the effect produced by forms in the light of psychological theories, see Estelle Thibault, *La Géométrie des émotions: Les Esthétiques scientifiques de l'architecture en France, 1850–1950* (Wavre: Mardaga, 2010).

11. Friedrich Kittler, *Gramophone, Film, Typewriter* [*Grammophon Film Typewriter,* 1986], trans. Geoffrey Winthrop-Young and Michael Wutz (Stanford, Calif.: Stanford University Press, 1999); Bernhard Siegert, *Cultural Techniques: Grids, Filters, Doors, and Other Articulations of the Real,* trans. Geoffrey Winthrop-Young (New York: Fordham University Press, 2015).

12. On Worringer's theories on the opposition between empathy and abstraction, see Papapetros, *On the Animation of the Inorganic.*

13. See especially Descartes's *Discours de la méthode* and *Méditations métaphysiques (Meditations on First Philosophy)* (1641).

14. Michael Baxandall, *Patterns of Intention: On the Historical Explanation of Pictures* (New Haven, Conn.: Yale University Press, 1985), 107.

15. Martyn Jolly, *Faces of the Living Dead: The Belief in Spirit Photography* (London: British Library, 2006).

16. See Julie Wosk, *Breaking Frame: Technology and the Visual Arts in the Nineteenth Century* (New Brunswick, N.J.: Rutgers University Press, 1992); Paul Dobraszczyk, *Iron, Ornament and Architecture in Victorian Britain: Myth and Modernity, Excess and Enchantment* (Burlington, Vt.: Ashgate, 2014).

17. The Egyptian vaults were described by the French engineer, historian, and archaeologist Auguste Choisy in the first volume of his monumental *Histoire de l'architecture* (Paris: Gauthier-Villars, 1899), as well as in another of his publications, *L'Art de bâtir chez les Égyptiens* (Paris: Édouard Rouveyre, 1904). Twentieth-century Egyptian architect Hassan Fathy introduced the ancient technique to a large public in search of modes of construction offering alternatives

to modernist concrete in *Gourna: A Tale of Two Villages* (Cairo: Ministry of Culture, 1969), which was republished under the more expressive title *Architecture for the Poor: An Experiment in Rural Egypt* (Chicago: University of Chicago Press, 1973).

18. Erwin Panofsky, "The Ideological Antecedents of the Rolls-Royce Radiator," *Proceedings of the American Philosophical Society* 107, no. 4 (August 1963): 273–88.

19. Michael Bell and Jeannie Kim, eds., *Engineered Transparency: The Technical, Visual, and Spatial Effects of Glass* (New York: Princeton Architectural Press, 2009).

20. See Brad Guy and Nicholas Ciarimboli, "Design for Disassembly in the Built Environment: A Guide to Closed-Loop Design and Building," Lifecycle Building Challenge, accessed August 19, 2019, http://www.lifecyclebuilding.org.

21. Whereas nineteenth-century scholars, often influenced by romantic conceptions, had a tendency to relate the construction of cathedrals from the perspective of the collective faith of their builders, the emphasis has shifted today toward the entrepreneurial activity developed by the cathedrals' sponsors. See, for instance, Alain Erlande-Brandenburg, *The Cathedral: The Social and Architectural Dynamics of Construction* [*La Cathédrale,* 1989], trans. Martin Thom (New York: Cambridge University Press, 2009).

22. I have developed this theme in Antoine Picon, "Universal Expositions, Utopias, and Architecture," in *The Companions to the History of Architecture,* vol. 3, *Nineteenth-Century Architecture,* ed. Martin Bressani and Christina Contandriopoulos (Chichester: John Wiley, 2017), 348–64.

23. Martin Pawley, *Buckminster Fuller* (London: Trefoil, 1990).

24. William R. Shea, *Galileo's Intellectual Revolution* (New York: Science History Publications, 1972).

25. James Graham Ballard, *Crash* (London: Jonathan Cape, 1973).

26. Jacques Proust, "L'Article 'Bas' de Diderot," in *Langue et langages de Leibniz à l'Encyclopédie,* ed. Michèle Duchet and Michèle Jalley (Paris: 10/18, 1977), 245–71.

27. Filippo Tommaso Marinetti, "Le Futurisme," *Le Figaro,* February 20, 1909, 1.

28. Le Corbusier, lecture given in Barcelona, March 30, 1932, C3-8-212-222, Archives de la Fondation Le Corbusier: "Le milieu séculaire des vitesses simples ne peut plus résister aux vitesses vingtuples."

29. See Tim Benton, *The Villas of Le Corbusier: 1920–1930* (New Haven, Conn.: Yale University Press, 1991).

30. Michael Osman, *Modernism's Visible Hand: Architecture and Regulation in America* (Minneapolis: University of Minnesota Press, 2018).

31. Reyner Banham, *The Architecture of the Well-Tempered Environment* (London: Architectural Press, 1969).

32. Antonio Damasio, *Self Comes to Mind: Constructing the Conscious Brain* (New York: Random House, 2010).

33. Lynn Hunt, *Writing History in the Global Era* (New York: W. W. Norton, 2014).

34. Tadao Ando, quoted in Kenneth Frampton, "Studies in Tectonic Culture: Reflections on the Scope of the Tectonic," in Foged and Hvejsel, *Tectonics in Architecture,* 158–59.

35. Le Camus, *Genius of Architecture,* 1: "l'analogie des proportions de l'architecture avec nos sensations"; Etienne-Louis Boullée, *Architecture: Essai sur l'art* [1780s] (Paris: Hermann, 1968).

36. Bruno Latour, *We Have Never Been Modern* [*Nous n'avons jamais été modernes: Essai d'anthropologie symétrique,* 1991], trans. Catherine Porter (Cambridge, Mass.: Harvard University Press, 1993), 10–11.

37. François Dagognet, interview by Roger-Pol Droit, published in *Le Monde,* 1993, republished in Roger-Pol Droit, *La Compagnie des contemporains: Rencontre avec des penseurs d'aujourd'hui* (Paris: Odile Jacob, 2002), 299.

38. Pierre Gros, "La Notion d'*ornamentum* de Vitruve à Alberti," *Perspective: La Revue de l'INHA* 2010–11, no. 1 (2010–11): 130–36, esp. 130–31; Ernst Hans Gombrich, *The Sense of Order: A Study in the Psychology of Decorative Art* (Ithaca, N.Y.: Cornell University Press, 1979).

39. Grabar, *Mediation of Ornament,* 193.

4. Architectural History and Regimes of Materiality

1. For an actor-network theory–oriented approach to the study of architecture, see Albena Yaneva, *Made by the Office for Metropolitan Architecture: An Ethnography of Design* (Rotterdam: 010 Publishers, 2009); Yaneva, *Mapping Controversies in Architecture.* On the prominence that media theory has recently acquired in the field of architectural history, it is worth looking at Mary Louise Lobsinger, "Architectural History: The Turn from Culture to Media," *Journal of the Society of Architectural Historians* 75, no. 2 (June 2016): 135–39.

2. See Picon, *Digital Culture in Architecture*; Mario Carpo, *The Alphabet and the Algorithm* (Cambridge: MIT Press, 2011).

3. Giulio Carlo Argan, "The Architecture of Brunelleschi and the Origins of Perspective Theory in the Fifteenth Century," *Journal of the Warburg and Courtauld Institutes* 9 (1946): 96–121.

4. Foucault, *The Order of Things.* On the role that monsters and wonders continued to play up to the time of the Enlightenment, see Lorraine Daston and Katharine Park, *Wonders and the Order of Nature, 1150–1750* (New York: Zone Books, 1998).

5. Michael Baxandall, *Painting and Experience in Fifteenth-Century Italy* (Oxford: Oxford University Press, 1972).

6. See, for example, David Hodes Friedman, "'Fiorenza': Geography and Representation in a Fifteenth Century City View," *Zeitschrift für Kunstgeschichte* 64, no. 1 (2001): 56–77. Friedman emphasizes the "tension between the medieval tradition of moralized geography and the new visual and scientific culture" of the Renaissance (58).

7. On this subject, see Szambien, *Symétrie, goût, caractère*, 131–40.

8. On the late medieval tendency to favor virtuosity, see Jean-Marie Guillouët, *Flamboyant Architecture and Medieval Technicality: The Rise of Artistic Consciousness and the End of Middle Ages (c. 1400–c. 1530)*, trans. Jane MacAvock (Turnhout: Brepols, 2019).

9. See, for example, Hilary Ballon and David Friedman, "Portraying the City in Early Modern Europe: Measurement, Representation, and Planning," in *The History of Cartography*, vol. 3, *Cartography in the European Renaissance*, ed. David Woodward (Chicago: University of Chicago Press, 2007), pt. 1, 680–704.

10. Mario Carpo and Francesco Furlan, eds., *Leon Battista Alberti's Delineation of the City of Rome (Descriptio urbis Romae)* (Tempe: Arizona Center for Medieval and Renaissance Studies, 2007).

11. Geoffrey Parker, *The Military Revolution: Military Innovation and the Rise of the West, 1500–1800* (Cambridge: Cambridge University Press, 1988).

12. Daniel Buisseret, ed., *Envisioning the City: Six Studies in Urban Cartography* (Chicago: University of Chicago Press, 1998).

13. Carl Havelange, *De l'œil et du monde: Une histoire du regard au seuil de la modernité* (Paris: Fayard, 1998).

14. Emil Kaufmann, *Von Ledoux bis Le Corbusier: Ursprung und Entwicklung der Autonomen Architektur* (Vienna: Passer, 1933).

15. Jean-Marie Pérouse de Montclos, *Étienne-Louis Boullée (1728–1799): De l'architecture classique à l'architecture révolutionnaire* (Paris: Arts et Métiers Graphiques, 1969); Michel Gallet, *Claude-Nicolas Ledoux, 1736–1806* (Paris: Picard, 1980); Anthony Vidler, *Claude-Nicolas Ledoux* (Cambridge: MIT Press, 1990); Daniel Rabreau, *Claude-Nicolas Ledoux (1736–1806): L'Architecture et les fastes du temps* (Bordeaux: William Blake, 2000).

16. For example, Vidler, *Writing of the Walls*.

17. On the question of solidity, see my discussion of the Panthéon dome in *French Architects and Engineers*.

18. Erika Naginski, *Sculpture and Enlightenment* (Los Angeles: Getty Research Institute, 2009), 290.

19. Stephen Timoshenko, *History of Strength of Materials, with a Brief Account of the History of Theory of Elasticity and Theory of Structures* (New York: McGraw-Hill, 1953).

20. See Bertrand Lemoine, *L'Architecture du fer: France XIXe siècle* (Seyssel: Champ Vallon, 1986).

21. Roberto Gargiani, *Concrete, from Archeology to Invention, 1700–1769: The Renaissance of Pozzolana and Roman Construction Techniques* (Lausanne: EPFL Press, 2013); André Guillerme, *Bâtir la ville: Révolutions industrielles dans les matériaux de construction, France-Grande-Bretagne 1760–1840* (Seyssel: Champ Vallon, 1995).

22. Lemoine, *L'Architecture du fer.*

23. Valérie Nègre, *L'Art et la matière: Les Artisans, les architectes et la technique (1770–1830)* (Paris: Classiques Garnier, 2016).

24. Antoine Picon, "Solidité et construction: Quelques aspects de la pensée constructive des Lumières," in *L'Idée constructive en architecture,* ed. Xavier Malverti (Paris: Picard, 1987), 73–106.

25. Ted Ruddock, *Arch Bridges and Their Builders, 1735–1835* (Cambridge: Cambridge University Press, 1979).

26. A. W. Skempton and H. R. Johnson, "The First Iron Frames," in *Structural Iron, 1750–1850,* ed. R. J. M. Sutherland (Burlington, Vt.: Ashgate, 1997), 19–44.

27. Condillac dedicated the last years of his life to working on a *langue des calculs* (language of calculations) that was inspired by this analogy.

28. Allison Muri, *The Enlightenment Cyborg: A History of Communications and Control in the Human Machine, 1660–1880* (Toronto: University of Toronto Press, 2007).

29. Picon, "Freestanding Column."

30. Pierre Jean Georges Cabanis, *Rapports du physique et du moral de l'homme* [1802] (Paris: Slatkine, 1980), 181.

31. Jean-Claude Perrot, *Une histoire intellectuelle de l'économie politique, XVIIe–XVIIIe siècle* (Paris: École des Hautes Études en Sciences Sociales, 1992).

32. Werner Szambien, *Jean-Nicolas-Louis Durand, 1760–1834: De l'imitation à la norme* (Paris: Picard, 1984); Antoine Picon, "From 'Poetry of Art' to Method: The Theory of Jean-Nicolas-Louis Durand," introduction to *Précis of the Lectures on Architecture* [*Précis des Leçons d'architecture,* 1802], by Jean-Nicolas-Louis Durand, trans. David Britt (Los Angeles: Getty Research Institute, 2000), 1–68.

33. Étienne Bonnot de Condillac, "Cours d'études pour l'instruction du prince de Parme" and "De l'art de penser," in *Œuvres philosophiques de Condillac,* 3 vols. (Paris: Presses Universitaires de France, 1947–51), 1 and 769.

34. This theorization notably came into play in relation to the question of the type of structure one should employ when using metal, a question on which Viollet-le-Duc disagreed with the architect Louis-Auguste Boileau. See the compilation of texts in Bernard Marrey, ed., *La Querelle du fer: Eugène*

Viollet-le-Duc contre Louis-Auguste Boileau (Paris: Linteau, 2002). Viollet-le-Duc later clarified his thinking in his *Discourses on Architecture.*

35. Antoine Picon, *L'Invention de l'ingénieur moderne: L'École des Ponts et Chaussées, 1747–1851* (Paris: Presses de l'École Nationale des Ponts et Chaussées, 1992).

36. Frank Lloyd Wright, "The Tyranny of the Skyscraper," in *Modern Architecture* (Princeton, N.J.: Princeton University Press, 1931), 85.

37. See, for instance, David Van Zanten, *Sullivan's City: The Meaning of Ornament for Louis Sullivan* (New York: W. W. Norton, 2000).

38. Cyrille Simonnet, *L'Architecture, ou La Fiction constructive* (Paris: Éditions de la Passion, 2001).

39. Sigfried Giedion, *Mechanization Takes Command: A Contribution to Anonymous History* (New York: Oxford University Press, 1948).

40. Simonnet, *Le Béton*; Forty, *Concrete and Culture.*

41. Sigfried Giedion, *Building in France, Building in Iron, Building in Ferroconcrete* [*Bauen in Frankreich, Bauen in Eisen, Bauen in Eisenbeton,* 1928], trans. J. Duncan Berry (Los Angeles: Getty Center for the History of Art and the Humanities, 1995).

42. David P. Billington, *Thin Shell Concrete Structures* (New York: McGraw-Hill, 1965).

43. See, for example, Jean-Louis Cohen, "Le Corbusier's Nietzschean Metaphors," in *Nietzsche and "An Architecture of Our Minds,"* ed. Alexandre Kostka and Irving Wohlfarth (Los Angeles: Getty Research Institute for the History of Art and the Humanities, 1999), 57–59.

44. See, for instance, Nicholas Fox Webber, *Le Corbusier: A Life* (New York: Alfred A. Knopf, 2008). With regard to Le Corbusier, the topic of eugenics is typically highlighted by those who see him as a member of the Fascist movement; they often fail to acknowledge, however, that interest in eugenics was a fundamental tendency of modernity, and hence widespread. Along these lines, see Christina Cogdell, *Eugenic Design: Streamlining America in the 1930s* (Philadelphia: University of Pennsylvania Press, 2010); Fabiola López-Durán, *Eugenics in the Garden: Transatlantic Architecture and the Crafting of Modernity* (Austin: University of Texas Press, 2018).

45. Beatriz Colomina, "X-Screens: Röntgen Architecture," *e-flux Journal,* no. 66 (October 2015), https://www.e-flux.com; Beatriz Colomina, "X-Ray Architecture: The Tuberculosis Effect," *Harvard Design Magazine,* no. 40 (Spring 2015): 74–93.

46. Neil Levine, *The Urbanism of Frank Lloyd Wright* (Princeton, N.J.: Princeton University Press, 2015).

47. See Christopher Hight, *Architectural Principles in the Age of Cybernetics* (New York: Routledge, 2008).

48. Pierre Gros, "Nombres irrationnels et nombres parfaits chez Vitruve," *Mélanges de l'École française de Rome: Antiquité* 88, no. 2 (1976): 669–704.

49. Françoise Choay, *The Rule and the Model: On the Theory of Architecture and Urbanism* [*La Règle et le modèle: Sur la théorie de l'architecture et de l'urbanisme*, 1980], trans. Denise Bratton (Cambridge: MIT Press, 1997); Pierre Caye, *Le Savoir de Palladio: Architecture, métaphysique et politique dans la Venise du Cinquecento* (Paris: Klincksieck, 1995).

50. Yves Pauwels, "Architecture, rhétorique et création littéraire au XVIe siècle," in *Repenser les limites: L'Architecture à travers l'espace, le temps et les disciplines*, ed. Alice Thomine-Berrada and Barry Bergdoll (Paris: INHA, 2005), https://journals.openedition.org/inha.

51. Mario Carpo, *Architecture in the Age of Printing: Orality, Writing, Typography, and Written Images in the History of Architectural Theory*, trans. Sarah Benson (Cambridge: MIT Press, 2001).

52. On the notion of license, see Mario Carpo, *La maschera e il modello: Teoria architettonica ed evangelismo nell'Extraordinario Libro di Sebastiano Serlio* (Milan: Jaca Book, 1993); Alina Payne, *The Architectural Treatise in the Italian Renaissance: Architectural Invention, Ornament, and Literary Culture* (Cambridge: Cambridge University Press, 1999).

53. David P. Billington, *The Tower and the Bridge: The New Art of Structural Engineering* (New York: Basic Books, 1983); Antoine Picon, ed., *L'Art de l'ingénieur, constructeur, entrepreneur, inventeur* (Paris: Éditions du Centre Pompidou, Le Moniteur, 1997).

54. Le Corbusier, "L'Espace indicible," in "Art," special issue, *L'Architecture d'Aujourd'hui* (April 1946): 9–17.

55. Alina Payne, *From Ornament to Object: Genealogies of Architectural Modernism* (New Haven, Conn.: Yale University Press, 2012).

56. Zevi, *Modern Language of Architecture*.

5. Architecture and Materiality in the Digital Era

1. See, in particular, Manuel De Landa, *A Thousand Years of Nonlinear History* (New York: Zone Books, 1997); Sanford Kwinter, *Far from Equilibrium: Essays on Technology and Design Culture* (Barcelona: Actar, 2007). On the notion of emergence in architecture, see Michael Weinstock, *The Architecture of Emergence: The Evolution of Form in Nature and Civilisation* (Chichester: John Wiley, 2010).

2. Greg Lynn, *Animate Form* (New York: Princeton Architectural Press, 1999).

3. On the early days of digital aspects in architecture, see in particular Picon, *Digital Culture in Architecture*, 15–57; Greg Lynn, ed., *Archaeology of the Digital: Peter Eisenman, Frank Gehry, Chuck Hoberman, Shoei Yoh* (Montreal: Canadian Centre for Architecture, 2013).

4. Bernard Tschumi, "Bernard Tschumi: I Believe in Placing Architecture in the Realm of Ideas and Invention," interview by Vladimir Belogolovsky, January 2004, Intercontinental Curatorial Project Inc., http://curatorialproject.com.

5. Greg Lynn, *Folds, Bodies, and Blobs: Collected Essays* (Brussels: La Lettre Volée, 1998). The term is an acronym for "binary large object," signifying a file format that contains the description of a geometric or multimedia object.

6. Frédéric Migayrou and Zeynep Mennan, eds., *Architectures non standard* (Paris: Éditions du Centre Pompidou, 2003).

7. Patrik Schumacher, *The Autopoiesis of Architecture,* vol. 1, *A New Framework for Architecture* (Chichester: John Wiley, 2011); Patrik Schumacher, *The Autopoiesis of Architecture,* vol. 2, *A New Agenda for Architecture* (Chichester: John Wiley, 2012).

8. Fabio Gramazio and Matthias Kohler, *The Robotic Touch: How Robots Change Architecture* (Zurich: Park Books, 2014).

9. "Contact," Gramazio Kohler Architects, accessed August 26, 2019, http://www.gramaziokohler.com.

10. Mario Carpo, *The Second Digital Turn: Design beyond Intelligence* (Cambridge: MIT Press, 2017).

11. On this subject, see James R. Beniger, *The Control Revolution: Technological and Economic Origins of the Information Society* (Cambridge, Mass.: Harvard University Press, 1986).

12. Sheila Jasanoff, ed., *States of Knowledge: The Co-production of Science and the Social Order* (New York: Routledge, 2004).

13. Stan Augarten, *Bit by Bit: An Illustrated History of Computers* (New York: Ticknor and Fields, 1984); Herman H. Goldstine, *The Computer: From Pascal to von Neumann* (Princeton, N.J.: Princeton University Press, 1993).

14. Edmund Callis Berkeley, *Giant Brains, or Machines That Think* (New York: John Wiley, 1949).

15. On the cybernetic view of the world, see Steve Joshua Heims, *Constructing a Social Science for Postwar America: The Cybernetics Group, 1946–1953* (Cambridge: MIT Press, 1991); Jean-Pierre Dupuy, *Aux origines des sciences cognitives* (Paris: La Découverte, 1994).

16. Antoine Picon, "Ordinateur/Computer/Numérique/Digital," in *Dictionary of Untranslatables: A Philosophical Lexicon,* ed. Barbara Cassin (Princeton, N.J.: Princeton University Press, 2014), 628.

17. Pierre Lévy, *La Machine univers: Création, cognition et culture informatique* (Paris: La Découverte, 1987), 124.

18. On the theme of the cyborg, see Donna Haraway, "Manifesto for Cyborgs: Science, Technology, and Socialist Feminism in the 1980s," *Socialist Review* 15, no. 2 (1985): 65–107; Chris Hables Gray, *The Cyborg Handbook* (New

York: Routledge, 1995); Paul N. Edwards, *The Closed World: Computers and the Politics of Discourse in Cold War America* (Cambridge: MIT Press, 1996); Antoine Picon, *La Ville territoire des cyborgs* (Besançon: Éditions de l'Imprimeur, 1998).

19. Raymond Kurzweil, *The Singularity Is Near: When Humans Transcend Biology* (New York: Penguin, 2005).

20. Gregory Bateson, *Steps to an Ecology of Mind: Collected Essays in Anthropology, Psychiatry, Evolution, and Epistemology* (San Francisco: Chandler, 1972).

21. Gilles Deleuze and Félix Guattari, *Anti-Oedipus: Capitalism and Schizophrenia* [*Capitalisme et schizophrénie: L'Anti-Oedipe,* 1973], trans. Robert Hurley, Mark Seem, and Helen R. Lane (Minneapolis: University of Minnesota Press, 1983); Gilles Deleuze and Félix Guattari, *A Thousand Plateaus: Capitalism and Schizophrenia* [*Capitalisme et schizophrénie: Mille plateaux,* 1980], trans. Brian Massumi (Minneapolis: University of Minnesota Press, 1987); Latour, *We Have Never Been Modern.*

22. Ingold, *Making,* 22. See also Sennett, *Craftsman.*

23. Spuybroek, *Sympathy of Things.*

24. Neil A. Gershenfeld, *Fab: The Coming Revolution on Your Desktop—from Personal Computers to Personal Fabrication* (New York: Basic Books, 2005).

25. Weinstock, *Architecture of Emergence.*

26. Georges Liaropoulos-Legendre, *ijp: The Book of Surfaces* (London, Architectural Association, 2003).

27. Papapetros, *On the Animation of the Inorganic.*

28. Carpo, *Second Digital Turn.*

29. On this subject, see in particular Jean Starobinski, *1789: The Emblems of Reason* [*1789: Les Emblèmes de la raison,* 1979], trans. Barbara Bray (Cambridge: MIT Press, 1988).

30. P. D. Anthony, *John Ruskin's Labour: A Study of Ruskin's Social Theory* (Cambridge: Cambridge University Press, 1983).

31. Antoine Picon, "Digital Fabrication, between Disruption and Nostalgia," in *Instabilities and Potentialities: Notes on the Nature of Knowledge in Digital Architecture,* ed. Chandler Ahrens and Aaron Sprecher (New York: Routledge, 2019), 223–38.

32. Gilles Deleuze, *The Fold: Leibniz and the Baroque* [*Le Pli: Leibniz et le baroque,* 1988], trans. Tom Conley (Minneapolis: University of Minnesota Press, 1992). This book's influence is particularly clear in the collection of essays that Greg Lynn assembled in 1993, *Folding in Architecture* (London: Wiley-Academy, 1993), a revised edition of which appeared in 2004.

33. Karl Chu, "Metaphysics of Genetic Architecture and Computation," in "Programming Cultures: Art and Architecture in the Age of Software," ed. Mike Silver, special issue, *Architectural Design* 76, no. 4 (July–August 2006): 38–45.

34. Marjan Colletti, *Digital Poetics: An Open Theory of Design-Research in Architecture* (Burlington, Vt.: Ashgate, 2013).

35. Christian Kerez, *Uncertain Certainty* (Tokyo: TOTO, 2013).

36. Addington and Schodek, *Smart Materials.*

37. On the differences between contemporary ornament and traditional ornament, see Picon, *Ornament.*

38. See Carpo, *Alphabet and the Algorithm.*

39. Iñaki Abalos and Renata Sentkiewicz, *Essays on Thermodynamics, Architecture and Beauty* (Barcelona: Actar, 2015).

40. Gilles Clément and Philippe Rahm, *Environ(ne)ment: Approaches for Tomorrow* (Milan: Skira, 2006); Philippe Rahm, *Architecture météorologique* (Paris: Archibooks, 2009).

41. See, for example, Kiel Moe, *Insulating Modernism: Isolated and Non-isolated Thermodynamics in Architecture* (Basel: Birkhäuser, 2014).

42. Torroja, *Les Structures architecturales,* 28.

43. Bernard Cache, *Objectile* (Orléans: HYX, 1998).

44. Lynn, *Animate Form,* esp. 26–28.

45. Mark Wigley, *The Architecture of Deconstruction: Derrida's Haunt* (Cambridge: MIT Press, 1997).

46. See, for example, Branko Kolarevic and Ali M. Malkawi, eds., *Performative Architecture: Beyond Instrumentality* (New York: Spon Press, 2005); Yasha Jacob Grobman and Eran Neuman, eds., *Performalism: Form and Performance in Digital Architecture* (New York: Routledge, 2012).

47. Bullivant, *Responsive Environments.*

48. Levit, "Contemporary 'Ornament.'"

49. Blaise Pascal, *The Miscellaneous Writings of Pascal,* trans. Georg Pearce (London: Longman, Brown, Green, and Longmans, 1849), 197.

50. See, for example, David Harvey, *The Ways of the World* (London: Profile Books, 2016).

51. Dagognet, interview, 299.

Conclusion

1. Barry Bergdoll, *Karl Friedrich Schinkel: An Architecture for Prussia* (New York: Rizzoli, 1994), 9.

2. See Manfredo Tafuri, *Architecture and Utopia: Design and Capitalist Development* [*Progetto e utopia: Architettura e sviluppo capitalistico,* 1973], trans. Barbara Luigia La Penta (Cambridge: MIT Press, 1976).

3. Benjamin, "Work of Art," 119.

4. Langdon Winner, "Do Artifacts Have Politics?," *Daedalus* 109, no. 1 (1980): 121–36. For a critique of Winner's argument, see Steve Woolgar and Geoff Cooper, "Do Artefacts Have Ambivalence? Moses' Bridges, Winner's

Bridges and Other Urban Legends in S&TS," *Social Studies of Science* 29, no. 3 (1999): 433–49.

5. Zevi, *Modern Language of Architecture.*

6. Albena Yaneva, *Five Ways to Make Architecture Political: An Introduction to the Politics of Design Practice* (London: Bloomsbury Academic, 2017).

7. Aggregate, *Governing by Design.*

8. See, for instance, Christian Norberg-Schulz, *Meaning in Western Architecture* (New York: Praeger, 1975); Juhani Pallasmaa, *The Thinking Hand*: Existential and Embodied Wisdom in Architecture (Chichester: John Wiley, 2009); Joseph Rykwert, *The Idea of a Town: The Anthropology of Urban Form in Rome, Italy and the Ancient World* (Princeton, N.J.: Princeton University Press, 1976).

9. Caye, *Empire et décor.*

10. Eve Blau, "Transparency and the Irreconcilable Contradictions of Modernity," *Praxis: Journal of Writing + Building,* no. 9 (2007): 50–59.

11. Temple Grandin, *Animals in Translation: Using the Mysteries of Autism to Decode Animal Behavior* (New York: Simon & Schuster, 2005).

12. On this key notion, see Flora Samuel, *Le Corbusier and the Architectural Promenade* (Basel: Birkhäuser, 2010).

13. Jean-Claude Schmitt, *Les Rythmes au Moyen Âge* (Paris: Gallimard, 2016).

14. Simon Sadler, *The Situationist City* (Cambridge: MIT Press, 1998); Mark Wigley, *Constant's New Babylon: The Hyper-architecture of Desire* (Rotterdam: Witte de With, Center for Contemporary Art/010 Publishers, 1998).

15. Jacques Rancière, *The Politics of Aesthetics* (London: Continuum, 2004).

16. An overview of the authors who have engaged this question can be found at the beginning of Schmitt, *Les Rythmes au Moyen Âge.*

17. For more on these topics, see Picon, *Ornament.*

18. Payne, *From Ornament to Object.*

Index

ANTOINE PICON is the G. Ware Travelstead Professor of the History of Architecture and Technology at Harvard Graduate School of Design. He is chairman of Fondation Le Corbusier. His books include *French Architects and Engineers in the Age of Enlightenment*; *Digital Culture in Architecture: An Introduction for the Design Professions*; *Ornament: The Politics of Architecture and Subjectivity*; and *Smart Cities: A Spatialised Intelligence*.